This book belongs to

Ishtar Breiber

First Poems

Compiled by Tig Thomas

Miles Kelly

First published in 2014 by Miles Kelly Publishing Ltd
Harding's Barn, Bardfield End Green, Thaxted, Essex, CM6 3PX, UK

This edition printed 2019

2 4 6 8 10 9 7 5 3 1

Publishing Director Belinda Gallagher
Creative Director Jo Cowan
Editorial Director Rosie Neave
Senior Editor Claire Philip
Designers Michelle Cannatella, Joe Jones, Jo Cowan, Venita Kidwai
Image Manager Liberty Newton
Production Elizabeth Collins, Jennifer Brunwin-Jones
Reprographics Stephan Davis, Callum Ratcliffe-Bingham
Assets Lorraine King

ISBN 978-1-78617-955-5

Printed in China

British Library Cataloguing-in-Publication Data
A catalogue record for this book is available from the British Library

ACKNOWLEDGEMENTS
The publishers would like to thank the following artists who have contributed to this book:
Cover: Julia Seal at Advocate
Inside pages:
Carly Gosnell, Frank Endersby, Kirsten Wilson
The Bright Agency: Mark Chambers, Richard Watson
Beehive Illustration: Rosie Brooks, Mike Phillips
All other artwork from the Miles Kelly Artwork Bank

The publishers would like to thank the following sources for the use of their photographs:
Fotolia.com 192 Dariusz Gudowicz **iStockphoto.com** 153 mcswin;
290 Stanislav Pobytov; 350 Andreas Kaspar; 372 Stanislav Pobytov
Shutterstock.com (paper background used throughout) Keattikorn; 154 & 155 Togataki

Made with paper from a sustainable forest

www.mileskelly.net

INTRODUCTION

This book is a treasure chest of words,
full of delightful poetry to suit all moods.
Some poems are very old, but they speak of
experiences that anyone can understand –
having a cold nose in winter or chasing
butterflies in the garden.

CONTENTS

FUN AND NONSENSE

ENCHANTED LANDS

ALL THE DAY LONG

A WONDERFUL WORLD

FUN AND NONSENSE

Some of these poems are just plain nonsense, others make sense but are delightfully funny. There are riddles to solve and limericks to laugh at, as well as some longer comical verses to puzzle and amaze.

The Triantiwontigongolope

There's a very funny insect that you do not often spy,
And it isn't quite a spider, and it isn't quite a fly;
It is something like a beetle, and a little like a bee,
But nothing like a woolly grub that climbs upon a tree.
Its name is quite a hard one, but you'll learn it soon, I hope.
So try:

"Tri-
Tri-anti-wonti-
Triantiwontigongolope"

Beetle-bee

Spider-fly

It lives on weeds and wattle-gum, and has a funny face;
Its appetite is hearty, and its manners a disgrace.
When first you come upon it, it will give you quite a scare,
But when you look for it again, you find it isn't there.
And unless you call it softly it will stay away and mope.
So try:

"Tri-
Tri-anti-wonti-
Triantiwontigongolope"

Wattle-gum
a sticky substance
from the trunk of
the wattle tree

Woolly grub

It trembles if you tickle it or tread upon its toes;
It is not an early riser, but it has a snubbish nose.
If you snear at it, or scold it, it will scuttle off in shame,
But it purrs and purrs quite proudly if you call it by its name,
And offer it some sandwiches of sealing-wax and soap.
So try:

"Tri-
Tri-anti-wonti-
Triantiwontigongolope"

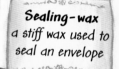

Sealing-wax
a stiff wax used to
seal an envelope

Snubbish nose

purr purr purr!

But of course you haven't seen it; and I truthfully confess
That I haven't seen it either, and I don't know its address.
For there isn't such an insect, though there really might have been
If the trees and grass were purple, and the sky was bottle green.
It's just a little joke of mine, which you'll forgive, I hope.
Oh, try!

"Tri-
Tri-anti-wonti-
Triantiwontigongolope"

C J Dennis

Sandwich-eater

The Poor Little Toe

I am all tired out, said the mouth, with a pout,
I am all tired out with talk.
Just wait, said the knee, till you're lame as you can be,
And then have to **walk — walk — walk.**

My work, said the hand, is the hardest in the land.
Nay, mine is harder yet, said the brain.
When you toil, said the eye, as steadily as I,
O then you'll have reason to complain.

Then a voice, faint and low, of the poor little toe
Spoke out in the dark with a wail:
It is seldom I complain, but you all will bear your pain
With more patience if you hearken to my tale.

I'm the youngest of five, and the others live and thrive,
They are cared for, and considered and admired.
I am overlooked and snubbed, I am pushed upon
   and rubbed,
I am always sick and ailing, sore and tired.

But I carry all the weight of the body, small or great,
Yet no one ever praises what I do,
I am always in the way, and 'tis I who have to pay
For the folly and the pride of all of you.

Then the mouth and the brain and the hand said, 'tis plain
Though troubled be our lives with woe,
The hardest lot of all, does certainly befall
The poor little, humble little toe,
The snubbed little, rubbed little toe.

Ella Wheeler Wilcox

Hearken listen

Some Puzzles

The Man in the Wilderness asked of me
"How many blackberries grow in the sea?"
I answered him as I thought good.
"As many red herrings as grow in the wood."

The Man in the Wilderness asked me why
His hen could swim, and his pig could fly.
I answered him briskly as I thought best.
"Because they were born in a cuckoo's nest."

The Man in the Wilderness asked me to tell
The sands in the sea and I counted them well.
Says he with a grin **"And not one more?"**
I answered him bravely, **"You go and make sure."**

Anonymous

The New Vestments

There lived an old man in the Kingdom of Tess,
Who invented a purely original dress;
And when it was perfectly made and complete,
He opened the door and walked into the street.

By way of a hat he'd a loaf of Brown Bread,
In the middle of which he inserted his head;
His Shirt was made up of no end of dead Mice,
The warmth of whose skins was quite fluffy and nice;
His Drawers were of Rabbit-skins, so were his Shoes;
His Stockings were skins, but it is not known whose;
His Waistcoat and Trousers were made of Pork Chops;
His Buttons were Jujubes and Chocolate Drops;

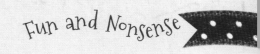

His Coat was all Pancakes, with Jam for a border,
And a girdle of Biscuits to keep it in order;
   And he wore over all, as a screen from bad weather,
   A Cloak of green Cabbage-leaves stitched all together.

   He had walked a short way, when he heard a
      great noise,
      Of all sorts of Beasticles, Birdlings, and Boys;
      And from every long street and dark lane in
         the town
      Beasts, Birdies, and Boys in a tumult rushed down.
   Two Cows and a Calf ate his Cabbage-leaf Cloak;
Four Apes seized his Girdle, which vanished
   like smoke;

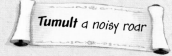

Tumult *a noisy roar*

Three Kids ate up half of his Pancaky Coat,
And the tails were devour'd by an ancient He Goat;
An army of Dogs in a twinkling tore up his
Pork Waistcoat and Trousers to give to their Puppies;
And while they were growling, and mumbling the Chops,
Ten Boys prigged the Jujubes and Chocolate Drops.
He tried to run back to his house, but in vain,
For scores of fat Pigs came again and again:
They rushed out of stables and hovels and doors;
They tore off his stockings, his shoes, and his drawers;
And now from the housetops with screechings descend
Striped, spotted, white, black, and grey Cats without end:
They jumped on his shoulders and knocked off his hat,
When Crows, Ducks, and Hens made a mincemeat of that;
They speedily flew at his sleeves in a trice,
And utterly tore up his Shirt of dead Mice;
They swallowed the last of his Shirt with a squall, –
Whereon he ran home with no clothes on at all.

Prigged stole

And he said to himself, as he bolted the door,
"I will not wear a similar dress any more,
Any more, any more, any more, never more!"

Edward Lear

The Cats have Come to Tea

What did she see – oh, what did she see,
As she stood leaning against the tree?
Why all the Cats had come to tea.

What a fine turn out – from
    round about,
All the houses had let
    them out,
And here they were with
    scamper and shout.

"Mew–mew–mew!" was all they could say,
    And, "We hope we find you well today."

Mew-mew-mew!

The Pelican Chorus

King and Queen of the Pelicans we;
No other Birds so grand we see!
None but we have feet like fins!
With lovely leathery throats and chins!

Ploffskin, Pluffskin, Pelican jee!
We think no Birds so happy as we!
Plumpskin, Ploshkin, Pelican jill!
We think so then, and we
**   thought so still!**

We live on the Nile. The Nile we love.
By night we sleep on the cliffs above;
By day we fish, and at eve we stand
On long bare islands of yellow sand.
And when the sun sinks slowly down,
And the great rock walls grow dark and brown,
Where the purple river rolls fast and dim
And the Ivory Ibis starlike skim,
Wing to wing we dance around,
Stamping our feet with a flumpy sound,
Opening our mouths as Pelicans ought;
And this is the song we nightly snort,

Ploffskin, Pluffskin, Pelican jee!
We think no Birds so happy as we!
Plumpskin, Ploshkin, Pelican jill!
We think so then, and we thought so still!

Last year came out our Daughter Dell,
And all the Birds received her well.
To do her honour a feast we made
For every bird that can swim or wade,
Herons and Gulls, and Cormorants black,
Cranes, and Flamingoes with scarlet back,
Plovers and Storks, and Geese in clouds,
Swans and Dilberry Ducks in crowds:
Thousands of Birds in wondrous flight!
They ate and drank and danced all night,
And echoing back from the rocks you heard
Multitude-echoes from Bird and Bird,

Ploffskin, Pluffskin, Pelican jee!
We think no Birds so happy as we!
Plumpskin, Ploshkin, Pelican jill!
We think so then, and we thought so still!

Yes, they came; and among the rest
The King of the Cranes all grandly dressed.
Such a lovely tail! Its feathers float
Between the ends of his blue dress-coat;
With pea-green trousers all so neat,
And a delicate frill to hide his feet
(For though no one speaks of it, every one knows
He has got no webs between his toes).
As soon as he saw our Daughter Dell,
In violent love that Crane King fell,
On seeing her waddling form so fair,
With a wreath of shrimps in her short white hair.
And before the end of the next long day
Our Dell had given her heart away;
For the King of the Cranes had won that heart
With a Crocodile's egg and a large fish-tart.
She vowed to marry the King of the Cranes,
Leaving the Nile for stranger plains;
And away they flew in a gathering crowd
Of endless birds in a lengthening cloud.

Ploffskin, Pluffskin,
   Pelican jee!
We think no Birds so happy as we!
Plumpskin, Ploshkin, Pelican jill!
We think so then, and we thought so still!

And far away in the twilight sky
We heard them singing a lessening cry,
Farther and farther, till out of sight,
And we stood alone in the silent night!
Often since, in the nights of June,
We sit on the sand and watch the moon,

She has gone to the great Gromboolian Plain,
And we probably never shall meet again!
Oft, in the long still nights of June,
We sit on the rocks and watch the moon,
She dwells by the streams of the Chankly Bore.
And we probably never shall see her more.

Ploffskin, Pluffskin, Pelican jee!
We think no Birds so happy as we!
Plumpskin, Ploshkin, Pelican jill!
We think so then, and we thought
so still!

Edward Lear

Jabberwocky

This poem sounds as if it is full of difficult words, but most of them are made up; they can mean whatever you want them to mean.

'Twas brillig, and the slithy toves
Did gyre and gimble in the wabe;
All mimsy were the borogoves,
And the mome raths outgrabe.

"Beware the Jabberwock, my son!
The jaws that bite, the claws that catch!
Beware the Jubjub bird, and shun
The frumious Bandersnatch!"

He took his vorpal sword in hand:
Long time the manxome foe he sought.
So rested he by the Tumtum tree,
And stood awhile in thought.

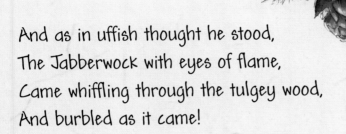

And as in uffish thought he stood,
The Jabberwock with eyes of flame,
Came whiffling through the tulgey wood,
And burbled as it came!

One, two! One, two! And through, and through
The vorpal blade went snicker-snack!
He left it dead, and with its head
He went galumphing back.

"And hast thou slain the Jabberwock?
    Come to my arms, my beamish boy!
     Oh, frabjous day! Callooh! Callay!"
    He chortled in his joy.

'Twas brillig, and the slithy toves
Did gyre and gimble in the wabe;
All mimsy were the borogoves
And the mome raths outgrabe.

Lewis Carroll

The Owl and the Pussy-cat

The Owl and the Pussy-cat went to sea
In a beautiful pea-green boat,
They took some honey, and plenty of money,
Wrapped up in a five-pound note.
The Owl looked up to the stars above,
And sang to a small guitar,
"Oh, lovely Pussy, oh, Pussy, my love,
What a beautiful Pussy you are,
You are,
You are!
What a beautiful Pussy you are!"

Pussy said to the Owl,
   "You elegant fowl,
How charmingly sweet you sing!
Oh, let us be married; too long we
   have tarried:
But what shall we do for a ring?"
They sailed away for a year and a day,
To the land where the bong-tree grows;
And there in the wood a Piggy-wig stood,
With a ring at the end of his nose,
His nose,
His nose,
With a ring at the end of his nose.

"Dear Pig, are you willing to sell for one shilling
Your ring?" Said the Piggy, "I will."
So they took it away and were married next day
By the Turkey who lives on the hill.
They dined on mince and slices of quince,
Which they ate with a runcible spoon;
And hand in hand, on the edge of the sand,
They danced by the light of the moon,
The moon,
The moon,
They danced by the light of the moon.

Edward Lear

Betty Botter Bought some Butter

Betty Botter bought some butter,
But, she said, this butter's bitter;
If I put it in my batter
It will make my batter bitter.
But a bit of better butter
Will make my batter better.

So she bought a bit of butter
Better than her bitter butter,
And she put it in her batter
And the batter was not bitter.
So, 'twas better Betty Botter
Bought a bit of better butter.

Anonymous

Buzz buzz buzz!

The Old Man in a Tree

There was an Old Man in a tree
Who was horribly bored by a bee;
When they said, "Does it buzz?"
He replied, "Yes, it does!
It's a regular brute of a bee!"

Edward Lear

Jerry Hall

Jerry Hall, he was so small,
A rat could eat him, hat and all.

Anonymous

Aiken Drum

There was a man lived in the moon,
Lived in the moon, lived in the moon
There was a man lived in the moon,
And his name was Aiken Drum.

And he played upon a ladle,
A ladle, a ladle,
And he played upon a ladle,
and his name was Aiken Drum.

And his hat was made of good cream cheese,
Of good cream cheese, of good cream cheese,
And his hat was made of good cream cheese
And his name was Aiken Drum.

And he played upon a ladle,
A ladle, a ladle,
And he played upon a ladle,
and his name was Aiken Drum.

And his coat was made of good
    roast beef,
Of good roast beef, of good
    roast beef,
And his coat was made of
    good roast beef,
And his name was
    Aiken Drum.

And he played upon a ladle,
A ladle, a ladle,
And he played upon a ladle,
and his name was Aiken Drum.

And his buttons made of penny loaves,
Of penny loaves, of penny loaves,
And his buttons made of penny loaves,
And his name was Aiken Drum.

And he played upon a ladle,
A ladle, a ladle,
And he played upon a ladle,
and his name was Aiken Drum.

And his breeches made of haggis bags
Of haggis bags, of haggis bags
And his breeches made of haggis bags,
And his name was Aiken Drum.

And he played upon a ladle,
A ladle, a ladle,
And he played upon a ladle,
and his name was Aiken Drum.

Anonymous

Calico Pie

Calico Pie,
The little Birds fly
Down to the calico tree,
Their wings were blue,
And they sang "Tilly-loo!"
Till away they flew, —
And they never came back to me!
They never came back!
They never came back!
They never came back to me!

Calico Jam,
The little Fish swam,
Over the syllabub sea,
He took off his hat,
To the Sole and the Sprat,
And the Willeby-Wat, —
But he never came back to me!
He never came back!
He never came back!
He never came back to me!

Calico Ban,
The little Mice ran,
To be ready in time for tea,
Flippity flup,
They drank it all up,
And danced in the cup, —
But they never came back to me!

They never came back!
They never came back!
They never came back to me!

Calico Drum,
The Grasshoppers come,
The Butterfly, Beetle, and Bee,
Over the ground,
Around and around,
With a hop and a bound, —
But they never came back to me!

They never came back!
They never came back!
They never came back to me!

Edward Lear

The Man who went Mad

There was a man and he went mad,
And he jumped into a biscuit bag;

The biscuit bag it was so full,
So he jumped into a roaring bull;

The roaring bull it was so fat,
So he jumped into a
gentleman's hat;

The gentleman's hat it was so fine,
So he jumped into a bottle of wine;

The bottle of wine it was so dear,
So he jumped into a barrel of beer;

The barrel of beer it was so thick,
So he jumped into a walking stick;

The walking stick it was so narrow,
So he jumped into a wheelbarrow;

The wheelbarrow began to crack,
So he jumped into a haystack;

The haystack began to blaze,
So he did nothing but cough and sneeze!

Anonymous

There was an Old Lady

There was an old lady who swallowed a fly
I don't know why she swallowed a fly – perhaps she'll die!

There was an old lady who swallowed a spider,

That wriggled and wiggled and tickled inside her,

She swallowed the spider to catch the fly;
I don't know why she swallowed a fly – perhaps she'll die!

There was an old lady who swallowed a bird;
How absurd to swallow a bird.
She swallowed the bird to catch the spider,
She swallowed the spider to catch the fly;
I don't know why she swallowed a fly – perhaps she'll die!

There was an old lady who swallowed a cat;
Fancy that to swallow a cat!
She swallowed the cat to catch the bird,
She swallowed the bird to catch the spider,
She swallowed the spider to catch the fly;
I don't know why she swallowed a fly – perhaps she'll die!

There was an old lady that swallowed a dog;
What a hog, to swallow a dog;
She swallowed the dog to catch the cat,
She swallowed the cat to catch the bird,
She swallowed the bird to catch the spider,
She swallowed the spider to catch the fly;
I don't know why she swallowed a fly – perhaps she'll die!

There was an old lady who swallowed a cow,
I don't know how she swallowed a cow;
She swallowed the cow to catch the dog,
She swallowed the dog to catch the cat,
She swallowed the cat to catch the bird,
She swallowed the bird to catch the spider,
She swallowed the spider to catch the fly;
I don't know why she swallowed a fly – perhaps she'll die!

There was an old lady who swallowed a horse,
She's dead, of course!

Anonymous

The Lady of Antigua

A lady there was of Antigua,
Who said to her spouse, "What a pig you are!"
He answered, "My queen
Is it manners you mean,
Or do you refer to my figure?"

G K Chesterton

The Young Lady of Norway

There was a Young Lady of Norway,
Who casually sat in a doorway;
When the door squeezed her flat,
she exclaimed "What of that?"
This courageous Young Lady
    of Norway.

Edward Lear

The Duck and the Kangaroo

Said the Duck to the Kangaroo,
"Good gracious! How you hop!
Over the fields and the water too,
As if you never would stop!
My life is a bore in this nasty pond,
And I long to go out in the world beyond!
I wish I could hop like you!"
Said the Duck to the Kangaroo.

"Please give me a ride on your back!"
Said the Duck to the Kangaroo.
"I would sit quite still, and say nothing but 'Quack,'
The whole of the long day through!
And we'd go to the Dee, and the Jelly Bo Lee,
Over the land, and over the sea;
Please take me a ride! O do!"
Said the Duck to the Kangaroo.

Said the Kangaroo to the Duck.
"This requires a little reflection;
Perhaps on the whole it might bring me luck,
And there seems but one objection,
Which is, if you'll let me speak so bold,
Your feet are unpleasantly wet and cold,
And would probably give me the roo–
Matiz!" said the Kangaroo.

Said the Duck, "As I sat on the rocks,
I have thought over that completely,
And I bought four pair of worsted socks
Which fit my web-feet neatly.
And to keep out the cold I've bought a cloak,
And every day a cigar I'll smoke,
All to follow my own dear true
Love of a Kangaroo!"

Said the Kangaroo, "I'm ready!
All in the moonlight pale,
But to balance me well, dear Duck, sit steady!
And quite at the end of my tail!"
So away they went with a hop and a bound,
And they hopped the whole world three time round;
And who so happy, O who,
As the Duck and the Kangaroo?

Edward Lear

The Cow and the Chicken

The chicken is a noble beast
The cow is much forlorner
Standing in the pouring rain
A leg on every corner.

Anonymous

A Ride

A farmer went riding upon his grey mare,

Bumpety, bumpety, bump!

With his daughter behind him so rosy and fair,

Lumpety, lumpety, lump

A raven cried, "Croak!" and they all tumbled down,

Bumpety, bumpety, bump!

The mare broke her knees and the farmer his crown,

Lumpety, lumpety, lump

The mischievous raven flew laughing away,

Bumpety, bumpety, bump!

And vowed he would serve them the same the next day,

Lumpety, lumpety, lump

Anonymous

Me and my Brother

In form and feature, face and limb,
I grew so like my brother,
That folks got taking me for him,
And each for one another.

It puzzled all our kith and kin,
It reached a fearful pitch;
For one of us was born a twin,
Yet not a soul knew which.

One day, to make the matter worse,
Before our names were fixed,
As we were being washed by nurse,
We got completely mixed;

And thus, you see, by fate's decree,
Or rather nurse's whim,
My brother John got christened me,
And I got christened him.

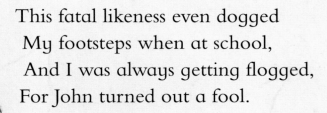

This fatal likeness even dogged
 My footsteps when at school,
 And I was always getting flogged,
For John turned out a fool.

 I put this question, fruitlessly,
 To everyone I knew,
"What would you do, if you were me,
To prove that you were you?"

 Our close resemblance turned the tide
 Of my domestic life,
  For somehow, my intended bride
  Became my brother's wife.

 In fact, year after year the same
 Absurd mistakes went on,
  And when I died, the neighbours came
  And buried brother John.

Henry S Leigh

A Dark Night

The night was growing old
As she trudged through snow and sleet;
Her nose was long and cold,
And her shoes were full of feet.

Anonymous

The Man in the Moon

The Man in the Moon as he sails the sky
Is a very remarkable skipper,
But he made a mistake when he tried to take
A drink of milk from the Dipper.
He dipped right out of the Milky Way,
And slowly and carefully filled it,
The Big Bear growled, and the Little Bear howled
And frightened him so that he spilled it!

Anonymous

Dipper a group of stars also called the Plough and the Saucepan

The Young Person in Green

There was a Young Person in green,
Who seldom was fit to be seen;
She wore a long shawl, over bonnet and all,
Which enveloped that person in green.

Edward Lear

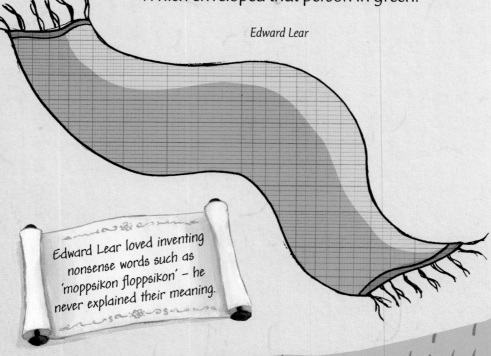

Edward Lear loved inventing nonsense words such as 'moppsikon floppsikon' – he never explained their meaning.

The Person of Ware

There was an Old Person of Ware,
Who rode on the back of a bear;
When they asked, "Does it trot?" he said, "Certainly not!
He's a Moppsikon Floppsikon bear!"

Edward Lear

Precocious Piggy

"Where are you going to, you little pig?"
"I'm leaving my Mother, I'm growing so big!"
"So big, young pig,
So young, so big!
What, leaving your Mother, you foolish young pig!"

"Where are you going to, you little pig?"
"I've got a new spade, and I'm going to dig."
"To dig, little pig?
A little pig dig!
Well, I never saw a pig with a spade that could dig!"

"Where are you going to, you little pig?"
"Why, I'm going to have a nice ride in
    a gig!"
"In a gig, little pig! What,
    a pig in a gig!
Well, I never saw a pig ride
    in a gig!"

"Where are you going to, you little pig?"
"Well, I'm going to the ball to dance a fine jig!"
"A jig, little pig!
A pig dance a jig!
Well, I never before saw a pig dance a jig!"

"Where are you going to, you little pig?"
"I'm going to the fair to run a fine rig."
"A rig, little pig!
A pig run a rig!
Well, I never before saw a pig run a rig!"

"Where are you going to, you little pig?"
"I'm going to the barber's to buy me a wig!"
"A wig, little pig!
A pig in a wig!
Why, whoever before saw a pig in a wig!"

Thomas Hood

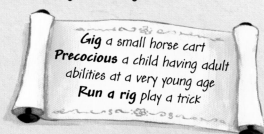

Gig a small horse cart
Precocious a child having adult
abilities at a very young age
Run a rig play a trick

Wouldn't it be Funny?

Wouldn't it be funny —
Wouldn't it, now —
If the dog said, "Moo-oo"
And the cow said, "Bow-wow"?
If the cat sang and whistled,
And the bird said, "Mia-ow"?
Wouldn't it be funny —
Wouldn't it, now?

Anonymous

Moo-oo

Mia-ow

BOW-WOW BOW-WOW
Bow-wow

MOO-OO MOO-OO

A Big Shoe

Said little Sue
To little Pete,
"I can't see you,
For your big feet."

Said little Pete
To little Sue
"'Tis not my feet,
'Tis but my shoe."

Anonymous

Tweedledum and Tweedledee

Tweedledum and Tweedledee
Resolved to have a battle
For Tweedledum said Tweedledee
Had spoiled his nice new rattle.

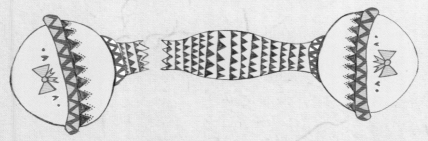

Just then flew by a monstrous crow
As big as a tar barrel,
Which frightened both the heroes so
They quite forgot their quarrel.

Anonymous

The Music of your Voice

A vase upon the mantelpiece,
    A ship upon the sea,
A goat upon a mountain-top
    Are much the same to me;
But when you mention melon jam,
    Or picnics by the creek,
Or apple pies, or pantomimes,
    I love to hear you speak.

Magna Carta an important document signed by the King of England in 1215

The date of Magna Carta or
  The doings of the Dutch,
Or capes, or towns, or verbs, or nouns
  Do not excite me much;
But when you mention motor rides –
  Down by the sea for choice
Or chasing games, or chocolates,
  I love to hear your voice.

C J Dennis

Amelia

Amelia mixed the mustard,
She mixed it good and thick:
She put it in the custard
And made her Mother sick,
And showing satisfaction
By many loud huzza
"Observe" she said "the action
Of mustard on Mamma."

A E Housman

Why?

There was a young maid who said, "Why
Can't I look in my ear with my eye?
If I give my mind to it,
I'm sure I can do it,
You never can tell till you try."

Anonymous

Robin the Bobbin

Robin the Bobbin, the big-bellied Ben,
He ate more meat than fourscore men;
He ate a cow, he ate a calf,
He ate a butcher and a half;
He ate a church, he ate
    a steeple,
He ate the priest and
    all the people!
A cow and a calf,
An ox and a half,
A church and a steeple,
And all the good people,
And yet he complained that his
    stomach wasn't full.

Anonymous

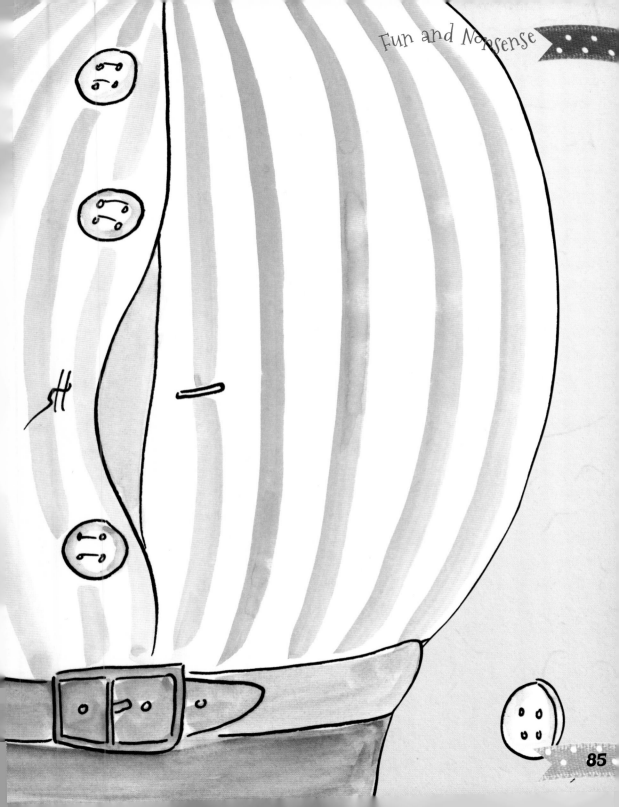

Fun and Nonsense

85

Mr Toad

The world has held great Heroes,
As history-books have showed;
But never a name to go down to fame
Compared with that of Toad!

The clever men at Oxford
Know all that there is to be
    knowed.
But they none of them know
    one half as much
As intelligent Mr Toad!

The animals sat in the Ark and
    cried,
Their tears in torrents flowed.
Who was it said, "There's land ahead?"
Encouraging Mr Toad!

The army all saluted
  As they marched along the road.
    Was it the King? Or Kitchener?
      No. It was Mr Toad.

      The Queen and her Ladies-in-waiting
        Sat at the window and sewed.
      She cried, "Look! Who's that HANDSOME man?"
They answered, "Mr Toad."

Kenneth Grahame

The Duel

The gingham dog and the calico cat
Side by side on the table sat;
'Twas half-past twelve, and (what do you think!)
Nor one nor t'other had slept a wink!
The old Dutch clock and the Chinese plate
Appeared to know as sure as fate
There was going to be a terrible spat.
(I wasn't there; I simply state
What was told to me by the Chinese plate!)

The gingham dog went

"BOW-WOW-WOW!"

And the calico cat replied

"Mee-ow!"

The air was littered, an hour or so,
With bits of gingham and calico,
While the old Dutch clock in the
   chimney place
Up with its hands before its face,
For it always dreaded a family row!
(Now mind: I'm only telling you
What the old Dutch clock declares is true!)

Gingham and calico are
two sorts of material.
The gingham dog and the
calico cat are stuffed toys.

The Chinese plate looked very blue,
And wailed, "Oh, dear! What shall we do!"
But the gingham dog and the calico cat
Wallowed this way and tumbled that,
Employing every tooth and claw
In the awfullest way you ever saw –
And, oh! How the gingham and calico flew!
 (Don't fancy I exaggerate –
I got my news from the Chinese plate!)

Next morning, where the two
   had sat
They found no trace of dog
   or cat;
And some folks think unto
   this day
That burglars stole that pair away!
But the truth about the cat and pup
Is this – they ate each other up!

"Mee-ow!"

Now what do you really think of that!
(The old Dutch clock it told me so,
And that is how I came to know.)

Eugene Field

ENCHANTED LANDS

Here you will read wonderful rhymes about fairies, goblins, witches, elves and even mermaids. This is the poetry of magic, enchanted lands, love and imagination.

Toot toot toot!

Elf Man

I met a little elf man, once,
  Down where the lilies blow.
I asked him why he was so small,
  And why he didn't grow.

He slightly frowned, and with his eye
  He looked me through and through.
"I'm quite as big for me," said he,
  "As you are big for you."

Anonymous

The Owl

When cats run home
  and light is come,
And dew is cold upon
  the ground,
And the far-off
  stream is dumb,
And the whirring
  sail goes round;
And the whirring sail goes round;
Alone and warming his five wits,
The white owl in the belfry sits.

When merry milkmaids click the latch,
And rarely smells the new-mown hay,
And the cock hath sung beneath the thatch
Twice or thrice his roundelay,
Twice or thrice his roundelay;
Alone and warming his five wits,
The white owl in the belfry sits.

Alfred, Lord Tennyson

Belfry bell tower
Roundelay a type of
song that repeats itself

The Elf and the Dormouse

Under a toadstool crept a wee Elf,
Out of the rain to shelter himself.

Under the toadstool, sound asleep,
Sat a big Dormouse all in a heap.

Trembled the wee Elf, frightened and yet
Fearing to fly away lest he get wet.

To the next shelter — maybe a mile!
Sudden the wee Elf smiled a wee smile.

Tugged till the toadstool toppled in two.
Holding it over him, gaily he flew.

Soon he was safe home, dry as could be.
Soon woke the Dormouse – "Good gracious me!"

"Where is my toadstool?" loud he lamented.
– And that's how umbrellas first were invented.

Oliver Herford

From Fairy King

"The breeze is on the Bluebells,
  The wind is on the leaf;
Stay out! Stay out! My little lad,
  And chase the wind with me.
If you will give yourself to me,
  Within the fairy ring,
    At deep midnight,
    When stars are bright,
You'll hear the Bluebells ring –

D!
DI! DIN!
DING!

On slender stems they swing.

"The rustling wind, the whistling wind,
 We'll chase him to and fro,
We'll chase him up, we'll chase him down
 To where the King-cups grow;
And where old Jack-o'-Lantern waits
 To light us on our way,
And far behind,
 Upon the wind,
The Bluebells seem to play –

D!
DI! DIN!
DING!

Lest we should go astray.

Juliana Horatia Ewing

Meg Merrilies

Old Meg she was a Gipsy,
     And liv'd upon the Moors:
Her bed it was the brown heath turf,
     And her house was out of doors.
Her apples were swart blackberries,
     Her currants pods o' broom;
Her wine was dew of the wild white rose,
     Her book a churchyard tomb.
Her Brothers were the craggy hills,
     Her Sisters larchen trees –
Alone with her great family
     She liv'd as she did please.
No breakfast had she many a morn,
     No dinner many a noon,
And 'stead of supper she would stare
     Full hard against the Moon.

But every morn of woodbine fresh
    She made her garlanding,
And every night the dark glen Yew
    She wove, and she would sing.
And with her fingers old and brown
    She plaited Mats o' Rushes,
And gave them to the Cottagers
    She met among the Bushes.
Old Meg was brave as Margaret Queen
    And tall as Amazon:
An old red blanket cloak she wore;
    A chip hat had she on.
God rest her aged bones somewhere –
    She died full long agone!

John Keats

Garlanding a flowery
ring or wreath
Woodbine honeysuckle

Jack Frost

Jack Frost is an imaginary creature who is said to paint patterns on windowpanes with frost.

The door was shut, as doors should be,
   Before you went to bed last night;
Yet Jack Frost has got in, you see,
   And left your window silver white.

He must have waited till you slept;
   And not a single word he spoke,
But pencilled o'er the panes and crept
   Away again before you woke.

And now you cannot see the hills
   Nor fields that stretch beyond the lane;
But there are fairer things than these
   His fingers traced on every pane.

Rocks and castles towering high;
   Hills and dales, and streams and fields;
And knights in armour riding by,
   With nodding plumes and shining shields.

And here are little boats, and there
   Big ships with sails spread to the breeze;
And yonder, palm trees waving fair
   On islands set in silver seas,

And butterflies with gauzy wings;
   And herds of cows and flocks of sheep;
And fruit and flowers and all the things
   You see when you are sound asleep.

For, creeping softly underneath
   The door when all the lights are out,
Jack Frost takes every breath you breathe,
   And knows the things you think about.

He paints them on the windowpane
   In fairy lines with frozen steam;
And when you wake you see again
   The lovely things you saw in dream.

Gabriel Setoun

Nine Little Goblins

They all climbed up on a high board-fence,
Nine little Goblins that had no sense,
Nine little Goblins, with green-glass eyes,
And couldn't tell coppers from cold mince pies;
    And they all climbed up on the
        fence, and sat,
        And I asked them what they
            were staring at.

        And the first one said, as he
            scratched his head
        With a queer little arm that
            reached out of his ear

And rasped its claws in his hair so red,
"This is what this little arm is for!"
And he scratched and stared, and the
    next one said,
"How on earth do you scratch
    your head?"

And he laughed like the
    screech of a rusty hinge,
Laughed and laughed till
    his face grew black;
And when he clicked, with a
    final twinge
Of his stifling laughter, he thumped
    his back
With a fist that grew on the end of his tail
Till the breath came back to his lips so pale.

And the third little Goblin
  leered round at me,
And there were no lids on his
  eyes at all
And he clucked one eye, and he
  says, says he,
"What is the style of your socks
  this fall?"
And he clapped his heels and I
  sighed to see
That he had hands where his feet
  should be.

Then a bald-faced Goblin, grey and grim,
Bowed his head, and I saw him slip
His eyebrows off, as I looked at him,
And paste them over his upper lip;
And then he moaned in remorseful pain,
"Would, ah, would I'd me brows again!"

And then the whole of the Goblin band
Rocked on the fence-top to and fro,
And clung, in a long row, hand in hand,
Singing the songs that they used to know,
Singing the songs that their grandsires sung
In the goo-goo days of the Goblin-tongue.

And ever they kept their green-glass eyes
Fixed on me with a stony stare,
Till my own grew glazed with a dread surmise,
And my hat whooped up on my lifted hair,
And I felt the heart in my breast snap to
As you've heard the lid of a snuff box do.

And they sang "You're asleep! There is no board-fence,
And never a Goblin with green-glass eyes!
"'Tis only a vision the mind invents
After a supper of cold mince pies,
And you're doomed to dream this way," they said,
"And you shan't wake up till you're clean plumb dead!"

James Whitcomb Riley

From Robin Hood

Yet let us sing
Honour to the old bow-string!
Honour to the bugle-horn!
Honour to the woods unshorn!
Honour to the Lincoln green!
Honour to the archer keen!
Honour to tight little John,
And the horse he rode upon!
Honour to bold Robin Hood,
Sleeping in the underwood!
Honour to maid Marian,
And to all the Sherwood clan!

John Keats

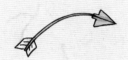

Minnie and Winnie

Minnie and Winnie
Slept in a shell.
Sleep, little ladies!
And they slept well.

Pink was the shell within,
Silver without;
Sounds of the great sea
Wandered about.

Sleep little ladies!
Wake not soon!
Echo on echo
Dies to the moon.

Two bright stars
Peep'd into the shell,
What are they dreaming of?
Who can tell?

Started a green linnet
Out of the croft;
Wake, little ladies,
The sun is aloft!

Alfred, Lord Tennyson

Croft a small farm building
Linnet a common small bird

Fairy Days

Beside the old hall-fire — upon my nurse's knee,
Of happy fairy days — what tales were told to me!
I thought the world was once — all peopled with
    princesses,
And my heart would beat to hear — their loves
    and their distresses;
And many a quiet night, — in slumber sweet
    and deep,
The pretty fairy people — would visit
    me in sleep.

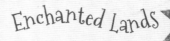

I saw them in my dreams – come flying east and west,
With wondrous fairy gifts – the new-born babe they bless'd;
One has brought a jewel – and one a crown of gold,
And one has brought a curse – but she is wrinkled and old.
The gentle queen turns pale – to hear those words of sin,
But the king he only laughs – and bids the dance begin.

The babe has grown to be — the fairest of the land
And rides the forest green — a hawk upon her hand.
An ambling palfrey white — a golden robe and crown;
I've seen her in my dreams — riding up and down;
And heard the ogre laugh — as she fell into his snare,
At the little tender creature — who wept and tore her hair!

But ever when it seemed — her need was at the sorest
A prince in shining mail — comes prancing through the forest.
A waving ostrich-plume — a buckler burnished bright;
I've seen him in my dreams — good sooth! a gallant knight.
His lips are coral red — beneath a dark moustache;
See how he waves his hand — and how his blue eyes flash!

"Come forth, thou Paynim knight!" — he shouts in accents clear.
The giant and the maid — both tremble his voice to hear.
Saint Mary guard him well! — he draws his falchion keen,
The giant and the knight — are fighting on the green.
I see them in my dreams — his blade gives stroke on stroke,
The giant pants and reels — and tumbles like an oak!

With what a blushing grace —
   he falls upon his knee

   And takes the lady's hand —
      and whispers, "You are free!"

   Ah! happy childish tales —
      of knight and faerie!

   I waken from my dreams —
      but there's ne'er a knight for me;

   I waken from my dreams —
      and wish that I could be

   A child by the old hall-fire —
      upon my nurse's knee."

William Makepeace Thackeray

Falchion a sort
of sword

Palfrey a horse
with a smooth pace

A Witch's Spell

Fillet of a fenny snake,
In the cauldron boil and bake;
Eye of newt, and toe of frog,
Wool of bat, and tongue of dog,

Adder's fork, and blind-worm's sting,
Lizard's leg, and howlet's wing,
For a charm of powerful trouble,
Like a hell-broth boil and bubble.

Double, double toil and trouble;
Fire burn and cauldron bubble...

Cool it with a baboon's blood
Now the spell is thick and good.

William Shakespeare

There were Three Sisters

There were three sisters fair and bright,
   Jennifer gentle and rosemary,
And they three loved one valiant knight.
   As the dew flies over the mulberry tree.

The eldest sister let him in,
   Jennifer gentle and rosemary,
And barred the door with a silver pin,
   As the dew flies over the mulberry tree.

The second sister made his bed,
   Jennifer gentle and rosemary,
And placed soft pillows under his head,
   As the dew flies over the mulberry tree.

The youngest sister, fair and bright,
Jennifer gentle and rosemary,
Was resolved for to wed with this valiant knight,
As the dew flies over the mulberry tree.

"And if you can answer questions three,
Jennifer gentle and rosemary,
O then, fair maid, I will marry with thee.
As the dew flies over the mulberry tree.

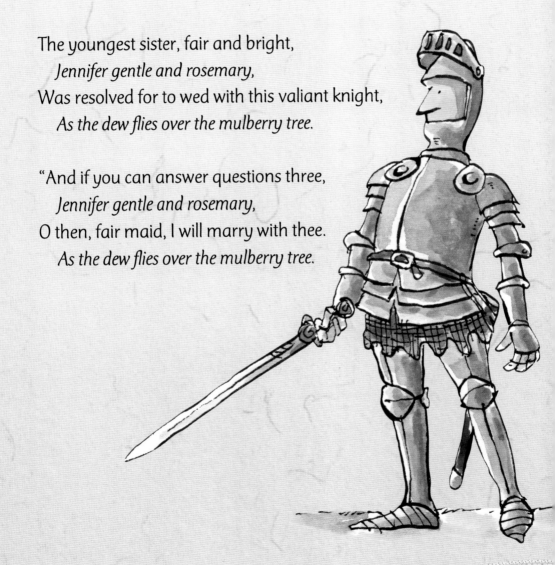

"What is louder than a horn,
　Jennifer gentle and rosemary,
And what is sharper than a thorn?"
　As the dew flies over the mulberry tree.

"Thunder is louder than a horn,
　Jennifer gentle and rosemary,
And hunger is sharper than a thorn."
　As the dew flies over the mulberry tree.

"What is broader than the way,
　Jennifer gentle and rosemary,
And what is deeper than the sea?"
　As the dew flies over the mulberry tree.

"Love is broader than the way,
  Jennifer gentle and rosemary,
And hell is deeper than the sea."
  As the dew flies over the mulberry tree.

"And now, fair maid, I will marry thee."

Anonymous

Boy-Dreams

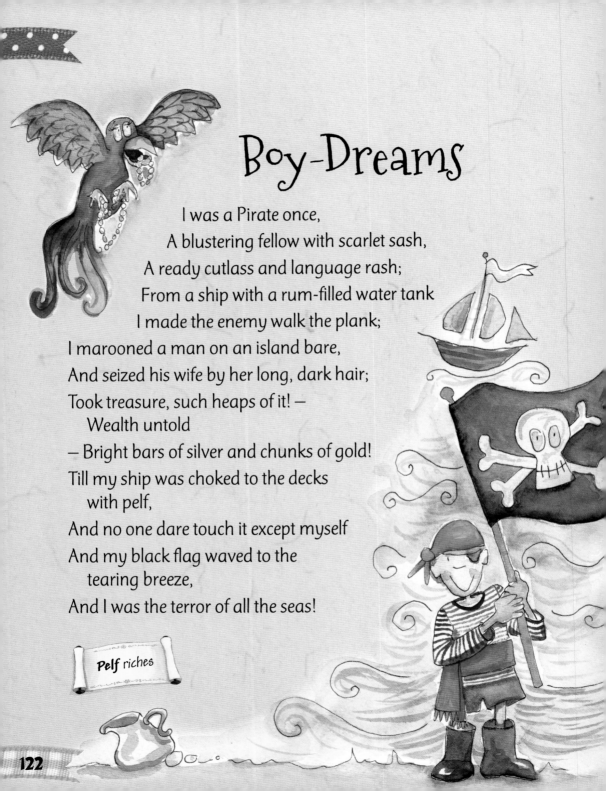

I was a Pirate once,
    A blustering fellow with scarlet sash,
    A ready cutlass and language rash;
    From a ship with a rum-filled water tank
    I made the enemy walk the plank;
I marooned a man on an island bare,
And seized his wife by her long, dark hair;
Took treasure, such heaps of it! —
    Wealth untold
— Bright bars of silver and chunks of gold!
Till my ship was choked to the decks
    with pelf,
And no one dare touch it except myself
And my black flag waved to the
    tearing breeze,
And I was the terror of all the seas!

Pelf riches

122

I was a Fairy once.
I swung in the bows of the
  silky oak,
And the harebells rang to the
  words I spoke,
And my wings were fashioned of silver
  gauze,
And I knew no grief and no human laws.
And I lived where the laces of green leaves
  sway.
And my life was one long, long holiday.
No tasks to learn, and no bothering rules,
No hectoring grown ups, and no — more — schools;
But a dance each eve, 'neath the moon's cold light,
To sit up as late as I liked at night.
For a lance I carried a grass-blade green,
And my shield was cut from an olivine;
I sipped cool dews from the cups of flowers,
My days were threaded of happy hours!

Olivine an olive-
coloured gemstone

I was a Merman once.
In the gloom of the amber-tinted seas,
With the brown tang clinging about my knees,
With a coral house, and a crab to ride,
Who pranced, and who ambled from side to side;
I wooed a Mermaid with emerald hair,
Dragged the fierce sea serpent from out his lair,
With his flaming tongue and his awful might,
And I slew him — easy — in open fight!
I had strings of pearls, white as frozen milk,
That were strung for me on sea-spider's silk;
And I never pined for the upper skies,
Whose blue came down in the dead men's eyes,
Drowned men with the salt on their blackened lips,
Who slid, drifting in, from the wrecks of ships;
But I took the gold from the belts of all,
To pave the road to my coral hall.

Tang *a coarse seaweed*

I was a Hunter once,
And I trapped and stalked in a pathless wood,
And the talk of the wild things understood.
With my leather leggings and hat of brown.
I tracked the elk and the redskin down;
Slew a grizzly bear in a mountain cave,
And tweaked the nose of an Indian brave.
Ere I shot the rapids in birch canoe —
For there was nothing I could not do.
There was naught I did not dare or enjoy,
In the magic world of a dreaming boy!

M Forrest

The Four Princesses

Four Princesses lived in a Green Tower —
    A Bright Green Tower in the middle of the sea;
And no one could think — oh, no one could think —
    Who the Four Princesses could be.

One looked to the North, and one to the South,
    And one to the East, and one to the West;
They were all so pretty, so very pretty,
    You could not tell which was the prettiest.

Their curls were golden — their eyes were blue,
    And their voices were sweet as a silvery bell;
And four white birds around them flew,
    But where they came from — who
        could tell?

Oh, who could tell? For no one knew,
   And not a word could you hear them say,
      But the sound of their singing, like church bells ringing,
         Would sweetly float as they passed away.

      For under the sun, and under the stars,
         They often sailed on the distant sea;
      Then in their Green Tower and Roses bower
         They lived again – a mystery.

   Kate Greenaway

The Land of Counterpane

When I was sick and lay a-bed,
I had two pillows at my head,
And all my toys beside me lay
To keep me happy all the day.

And sometimes for an hour or so
I watched my leaden soldiers go,
With different uniforms and drills,
Among the bed clothes, through
    the hills;

And sometimes sent my ships in fleets
All up and down among the sheets;
    Or brought my trees and houses out,
    And planted cities all about.

    I was the giant great and still
That sits upon the pillow-hill,
    And sees before him, dale and plain,
    The pleasant land of counterpane.

Robert Louis Stevenson

Wynken, Blynken and Nod

Wynken, Blynken, and Nod one night
Sailed off in a wooden shoe –
Sailed on river of crystal light,
Into a sea of dew.
"Where are you going, and what do you wish?"
The old moon asked the three.
"We have come to fish for the herring-fish
That live in this beautiful sea;
Nets of silver and gold have we!"
Said Wynken,
Blynken,
And Nod.

The old moon laughed and sang a song,
As they rocked in the wooden shoe,
And the wind that sped them all night long
Ruffled the waves of dew.
The little stars were the herring-fish
That lived in that beautiful sea –
"Now cast your nets wherever you wish
But never a feared are we";
   So cried the stars to the fishermen three:
      Wynken,
      Blynken,
      And Nod.

All night long their nets they threw
To the stars in the twinkling foam –
Then down from the skies came the wooden
  shoe,
Bringing the fishermen home;
'Twas all so pretty a sail, it seemed
As if it could not be,
And some folks thought 'twas a dream they'd
  dreamed
Of sailing that beautiful sea
But I shall name you the fishermen three:
Wynken,
Blynken,
And Nod.

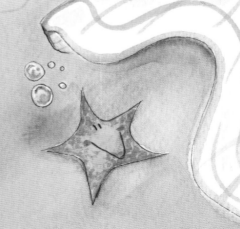

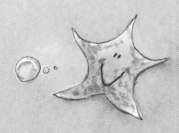

Wynken and Blynken are two little eyes,
And Nod is a little head,
And the wooden shoe that sailed the skies
Is a wee one's trundle-bed.
So shut your eyes while mother sings
Of wonderful sights that be,
And you shall see the beautiful things
As you rock on the misty sea,
Where the old shoe rocked the fishermen three:
Wynken,
Blynken,
And Nod.

Eugene Field

A Fairy's Song

Where the bee sucks, there suck I;
In the cowslip's bell I lie;
There I couch when owls do cry
On the bat's back I do fly
After summer, merrily:
Merrily, merrily shall I live now,
Under the blossom that hangs on the bough.

William Shakespeare

Couch lie

Queen Mab

A little fairy comes at night,
Her eyes are blue, her hair is brown,
With silver spots upon her wings,
And from the moon she flutters down.

She has a little silver wand,
And when a good child goes to bed
She waves her wand from right to left,
And makes a circle round its head.

And then it dreams of pleasant things,
Of fountains filled with fairy fish,
And trees that bear delicious fruit
And bow their branches at a wish.

Of arbours filled with dainty scents
From lovely flowers that never fade;
Bright flies that glitter in the sun,
And glow-worms shining in the shade:

And talking birds with gifted tongues,
For singing songs and telling tales,
And pretty dwarfs to show the way
Through fairy hills and fairy dales.

But when a bad child goes to bed,
From left to right she weaves her rings,
And then it dreams all through the night
Of only ugly, horrid things!

Then lions come with glaring eyes,
And tigers growl, a dreadful noise,
And ogres draw their cruel knives,
To shed the blood of girls and boys.

Then stormy waves rush on to drown,
Or raging flames come scorching round,
Fierce dragons hover in the air,
And serpents crawl along the ground.

Then wicked children wake and weep,
And wish the long black gloom away;
But good ones love the dark, and find
The night as pleasant as the day.

Thomas Hood

A Prince

A daring prince, of the realm Rangg Dhune,
Once went up in a big balloon
That caught and stuck on the horns of the moon,
And he hung up there till next day noon —
When all at once he exclaimed, **"Hoot-toot!"**
And then came down in his parachute.

James Whitcomb Riley

Climbing

High up in the apple tree climbing I go,
With the sky above me, the Earth below.
Each branch is the step of a wonderful stair
Which leads to the town I see shining up there.

Climbing, climbing, higher and higher,
The branches blow and I see a spire,
The gleam of a turret, the glint of a dome,

All sparkling and bright, like white sea foam.
On and on, from bough to bough,
The leaves are thick, but I push my way through;
Before, I have always had to stop,
But today I am sure I shall reach the top.

Today to the end of the marvellous stair,
   Where those glittering pinacles flash in the air!
      Climbing, climbing, higher I go,
         With the sky close above me, the earth far below.

Amy Lowell

Terence McDiddler

Terence McDiddler,
The three-stringed fiddler,
Can charm, if you please,
The fish from the seas.

Anonymous

A Fairy in Armour

He put his acorn helmet on;
It was plumed of the silk of the
    thistle down;
The corslet plate that guarded his
    breast
Was once the wild bee's golden vest;
His cloak, of a thousand mingled dyes,
Was formed of the wings of butterflies;
His shield was the shell of a lady-bird green,
Studs of gold on a ground of green;
And the quivering lance which he brandished
    bright,
Was the sting of a wasp he had slain in fight.

Joseph Rodman Drake

From The Crystal Cabinet

The maiden caught me in the wild,
Where I was dancing merrily;
She put me into her Cabinet,
And lock'd me up with a golden key.

This Cabinet is form'd of gold
And pearl and crystal shining bright,
And within it opens into a world
And a little lovely moony night.

Another England there I saw,
Another London with its Tower,
Another Thames and other hills,
And another pleasant Surrey bower.

William Blake

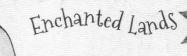

Sea Shell

Sea Shell, Sea Shell,

Sing me a song, O Please!
A song of ships, and sailor men,
And parrots, and tropical trees,
Of islands lost in the Spanish Main
Which no man ever may find again,
Of fishes and corals under the waves,
And seahorses stabled in great green caves.

Sea Shell, Sea Shell,

Sing of the things you know so well.

Amy Lowell

Mr Nobody

I know a funny little man,
As quiet as a mouse,
Who does the mischief that is done
In everybody's house!
There's no one ever sees his face,
And yet we all agree
That every plate we break was cracked
By Mr Nobody.

'Tis he who always tears our books,
Who leaves the door ajar,
Who pulls the buttons from our shirts,
And scatters pins afar;
That squeaking door will always squeak
For, prithee, don't you see,
We leave the oiling to be done
By Mr Nobody.

He puts damp wood upon the fire,
That kettles cannot boil;
His are the feet that bring in mud,
And all the carpets soil.
The papers always are mislaid,
Who had them last but he?
There's no one tosses them about
But Mr Nobody.

The finger marks upon the door
By none of us are made;
We never leave the blinds unclosed,
To let the curtains fade.
The ink we never spill, the boots
That lying round you see,
Are not our boots; they all belong
To Mr Nobody.

Anonymous

From The Mermaid

Who would be
A mermaid fair,
Singing alone,
Combing her hair
Under the sea,
In a golden curl
With a comb of
  pearl,
On a throne?

I would be a
  mermaid fair;
I would sing to myself the
  whole of the day;
With a comb of pearl I
  would comb my hair;
And still as I comb'd I
  would sing and say,
Who is it loves me? who loves not me?
I would comb my hair till my ringlets would fall
Low adown, low adown,

From under my starry sea-bud crown
Low adown and around,
And I should look like a fountain of gold
Springing alone
With a shrill inner sound,
Over the throne
In the midst of the hall;
Till that great sea snake under the sea
From his coiled sleeps in the central deeps
Would slowly trail himself sevenfold
Round the hall where I sate, and look in at the gate
With his large calm eyes for the love of me.
And all the mermen under the sea
　　Would feel their immortality
　　　　Die in their hearts for the love of me.

Alfred, Lord Tennyson

The Merman

Who would be
A merman bold,
Sitting alone,
Singing alone
Under the sea,
With a crown of gold,
On a throne?

I would be a merman bold,
I would sit and sing the whole of the day;
I would fill the sea-halls with a voice of power;
But at night I would roam abroad and play
With the mermaids in and out of the rocks,
Dressing their hair with the white sea-flower;

And holding them back by their flowing locks
I would kiss them often under the sea,
And kiss them again till they kiss'd me
Laughingly, laughingly;
And then we would wander away, away
To the pale-green sea-groves straight and high,
Chasing each other merrily.

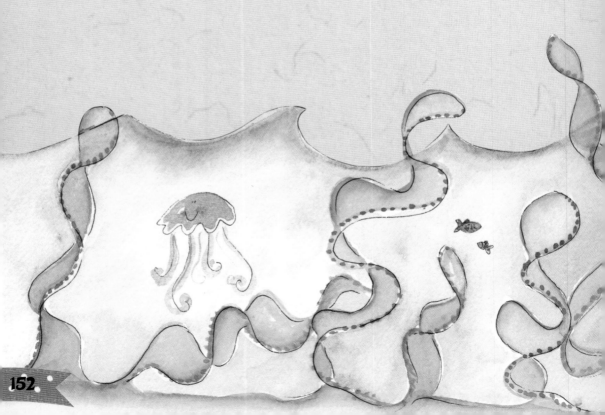

There would be neither moon nor star;
But the wave would make music above us afar –
Low thunder and light in the magic night –
Neither moon nor star…

Oh! What a happy life were mine
Under the hollow-hung ocean green!
Soft are the moss-beds under the sea;
We would live merrily, merrily.

Alfred, Lord Tennyson

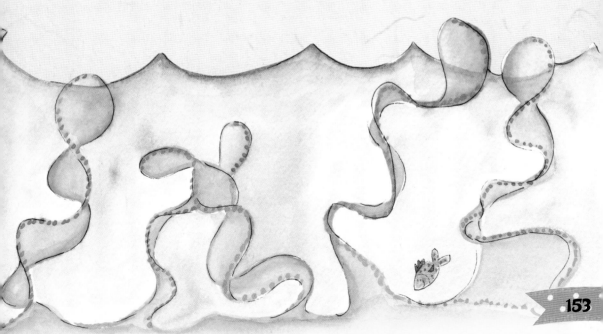

From The Butterfly's Ball and the Grasshopper's Feast

Come take up your Hats, and away let us haste
To the Butterfly's Ball, and the Grasshopper's Feast.
The Trumpeter, Gadfly, has summon'd the Crew,
And the Revels are now only waiting for you.

And there was the Gnat and the Dragonfly too,
With all their Relations, Green, Orange, and Blue.
And there came the Moth, with his Plumage of Down,
And the Hornet in Jacket of Yellow and Brown;

Who with him the Wasp, his Companion, did bring,
But they promis'd, that Evening, to lay by their Sting.
And the sly little Dormouse crept out of his Hole,
And brought to the Feast his blind Brother, the Mole.

And the Snail, with his Horns peeping out of his Shell,
Came from a great Distance, the Length of an Ell.
A Mushroom their Table, and on it was laid
Water-dock Leaf, which a Tablecloth made.

William Roscoe

Ell an old measurement, about the length of a man's arm

My Fairy

I have a fairy by my side
Which says I must not sleep,
When once in pain I loudly cried
It said **"You must not weep."**

If, full of mirth, I smile and grin,
It says **"You must not laugh;"**
When once I wished to drink some gin
It said **"You must not quaff."**

When once a meal I wished to taste
It said **"You must not bite,"**
When to the wars I went in haste
It said **"You must not fight."**

"What may I do?" at length I cried,
Tired of the painful task.
The fairy quietly replied,
And said **"You must not ask."**

Moral: **"You mustn't"**

Lewis Carroll

From Fairy Feast

Upon a mushroom's head
Our tablecloth we spread;
A grain of rye, or wheat,
Is manchet, which we eat;
Pearly drops of dew we drink
In acorn cups fill'd to the brink.

The brains of nightingales,

With unctuous fat of snails,

Between two cockles stew'd,

Is meat that's easily chew'd;

Tails of worms, and marrow of mice,

Do make a dish that's wondrous nice.

Anonymous

Manchet a loaf of
fine white bread

Unctuous oily

From The Noon Call

Sprightly, lightly,
Sing we rightly!
Moments brightly hurry away!
Fruit-tree blossoms,
And roses' bosoms
Clear blue sky of a summer day!
Dear blue sky of a summer day!

Springlets, brooklets,
Greeny nooklets,
Hill and valley, and salt-sea spray!
Comrade rovers,
Fairy lovers,
All the length of a summer day!
All the livelong summer day!

William Allingham

From Two Fairies in a Garden

O, far away,
Over river must we fly,
Over the sea and the mountain high,
Over city, seen afar
Like a low and misty star,
Soon beneath us glittering
Like million spark-worms. But our wing,
For the flight will ne'er suffice.
Some are training Flittermice,
I a Silver Moth."

William Allingham

Flittermice bats
Suffice be enough

The Fairy Pigwiggin Arms for the Fight

A little cockle-shell his shield,
Which he could very bravely wield,

Yet could it not be pierced –
His spear a bent both stiff and strong
And well-near of two inches long,
The pile was of a housefly's tongue
Whose sharpness naught reversed.

And puts him on a coat of mail,
Which was of a fish's scale,
That when his foe should him assail

No point should be prevailing:
His rapier was a hornet's sting,
It was a very dangerous thing;
For if he chanced to hurt the King
It would be long in healing.

Bent a stiff grass-stalk
Mettle courage
Pile the pointed metal head of spear
Rapier sharply pointed sword

His helmet was a beetle's head,
Most horrible and full of dread,
That able was to strike one dead,

Yet did it well become him;
And for a plume a horse's hair,
Which, being tossed with the air,
Had force to strike his foe with fear

And turn his weapon from him.
Himself he on an earwig set,
Yet scarce he on his back could get,
So oft and high he did curvet
Ere he himself could settle:

He made him turn and stop and bound,
To gallop and to trot the round;
He scarce could stand on any ground,
He was so full of mettle.

Michael Drayton

The Elves' Goodbye

The moonlight fades from flower and tree,
And the stars dim one by one;
The tale is told, the song is sung,
And the Fairy feast is done.
The night-wind rocks the sleeping flowers,
And sings to them, soft and low.
The early birds erelong will wake –
'Tis time for the Elves to go.

O'er the sleeping earth we silently pass,
Unseen by mortal eye,
And send sweet dreams, as we lightly float
Through the quiet moonlit sky;
For the stars' soft eyes alone may see,
And the flowers alone may know,
The feasts we hold, the tales we tell –
So 'tis time for the Elves to go.

From bird, and blossom, and bee,
We learn the lessons they teach;
And seek, by kindly deeds, to win
A loving friend in each.
And though unseen on earth we dwell,
Sweet voices whisper low,
And gentle hearts most joyously greet
The Elves where'er they go.

When next we meet in the Fairy dell,
May the silver moon's soft light
Shine then on faces gay as now,
And Elfin hearts as light.
Now spread each wing, for the eastern sky
With sunlight soon will glow.
The morning star shall light us home –
Farewell! For the Elves must go.

Louisa M Alcott

The Last Voyage of the Fairies

Down the bright stream the Fairies float,
A water lily is their boat.

Long rushes they for paddles take,
Their mainsail of a bat's wing make;

The tackle is of cobwebs neat,
With glowworm lantern all's complete.

So down the broad'ning stream they float,
With Puck as pilot of the boat.

The Queen on speckled moth-wings lies,
And lifts at times her languid eyes

To mark the green and mossy spots
Where bloom the blue forget-me-nots –

Oberon, on his rosebud throne,
Claims the fair valley as his own –

And elves and fairies, with a shout
Which may be heard a yard about,

Hail him as Elfland's mighty King;
And hazelnuts in homage bring,

And bend the unreluctant knee,
And wave their wands in loyalty.

Down the broad stream the Fairies float,
An unseen power impels their boat;

The banks fly past – each wooded scene –
The elder copse – the poplars green –

And soon they feel the briny breeze
With salt and savour of the seas –

Still down the stream the Fairies float,
An unseen power impels their boat;

Until they mark the rushing tide
Within the estuary wide.

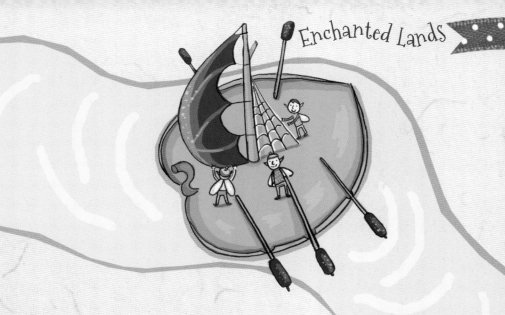

And now they're tossing on the sea,
Where waves roll high, and winds blow free,

Ah, mortal vision nevermore
Shall see the Fairies on the shore,

Or watch upon a summer night
Their mazy dances of delight!

Far, far away upon the sea,
The waves roll high, the breeze blows free!

The Queen on speckled moth-wings lies,
Slow gazing with a strange surprise

Where swim the sea-nymphs on the tide
Or on the backs of dolphins ride –

The King, upon his rosebud throne,
Pales as he hears the waters moan;

The elves have ceased their sportive play,
Hushed by the slowly sinking day –

And still afar, afar they float,
The Fairies in their fragile boat,

Further and further from the shore,
And lost to mortals evermore!

W H Davenport Adams

Good Luck Befriend Thee

Good luck befriend thee, Son; for at thy birth
The faery ladies danced upon the hearth.
The drowsy nurse hath sworn she did them spy
Come tripping to the room where thou didst lie,
And, sweetly singing round about thy bed,
Strew all their blessings on thy sleeping head.

John Milton

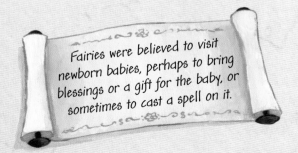

Fairies were believed to visit
newborn babies, perhaps to bring
blessings or a gift for the baby, or
sometimes to cast a spell on it.

An Elf Singing

An **Elf** sat on a twig,
He was not very big,
He sang a little song,
He did not think it wrong;
But he was on a Wizard's ground,
Who hated all sweet sound.

Elf, Elf,
Take care of yourself,
He's coming behind you,
To seize you and bind you
And stifle your song.

The Wizard! the Wizard!
He changes his shape
In crawling along,
An ugly old ape,
A poisonous lizard,
A spotted spider,
A wormy glider,

The Wizard! the Wizard!
He's up on the bough,
He'll bite through your gizzard,
He's close to you now!

The **Elf** went on with his song,
It grew more clear and strong,
It lifted him in the air,
He floated singing away,
With rainbows in his hair;
While the Wizard-worm from his creep
Made a sudden leap,
Fell down into a hole,
And, ere his magic word he could say,
Was eaten up by a Mole.

William Allingham

I Asked the Little Boy who Cannot See

I asked the little boy who cannot see,
"And what is colour like?"
"Why, green," said he,
"Is like the rustle when the wind blows through
The forest; running water, that is blue;
And red is like a trumpet sound; and pink
Is like the smell of roses; and I think
That purple must be like a thunderstorm;
And yellow is like something soft and warm;
And white is a pleasant stillness when you lie
And dream."

Anonymous

The Mermaid
and the Sailor Boy

There was a gallant sailor-boy who'd crossed the harbour bar
And sailed in many a foreign main — in fact he was a tar;
And leaning o'er the good ship's side into the deep looked he
When a skimpy little mermaid came swimming o'er the sea.
She was very scaly, and sang in every scale;
And then she cried "Encore! Encore!" and wagged her little tail
Till she came to the good ship's side, and saw the sailor-boy above
And a pang shot through her little heart, for she found she was in love.
She opened conversation, very cleverly, she thought.
"Have you spliced the capstan-jib, my boy? Is the tarpaulin taut?"
The sailor-boy was candid, he let his mirth appear —
He did not strive to hide his smile — he grinned from ear to ear.

She noticed his amusement, and it gave her feelings pain,
And her tail grew still more skimpy, as she began again.
"Oh, will you come and live with me? And you shall have delight
In catching limpets all the day and eating them all night;
And lobsters in abundance in the palace where I am;
And I will come and be thy bride, and make thee seaweed jam."
The sailor-boy did shut one eye, and then did it unclose;
And with solemnity he put his thumb unto his nose;
And said "Be bothered if I do, however much you sing;
You flabby little, dabby little, wetty little thing."

A E Housman

Tar sailor

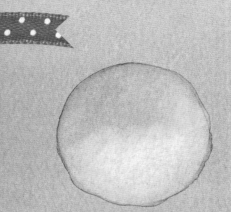

From The Gipsies

The fairy beam upon you,

The stars to glisten on you,

A moon of light

In the noon of night,

Till the firedrake hath o'er-gone you.

The wheel of fortune guide you,

The boy with the bow beside you

Run aye in the way

Till the bird of day

And the luckier lot betide you.

Ben Jonson

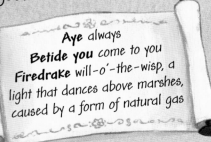

Aye always
Betide you come to you
Firedrake will-o'-the-wisp, a
light that dances above marshes,
caused by a form of natural gas

A Song for Scaring Goblins Away

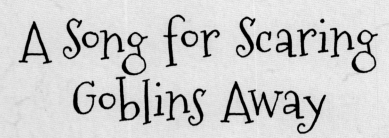

One, two –
Hit and Hew!
Three, four –
Blast and bore!
Five, six –
There's a fix!
Seven, eight –
Hold it straight!
Nine, ten –
Hit again
Hurry! Scurry!
Bother! Smother!

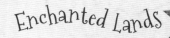

There's a toad
In the road!
Smash it!
Squash it!
Fry it!
Dry it!
You're another!
Up and off!
There's enough – **Huuuuuh!**

George Macdonald

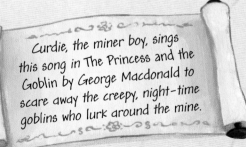

Curdie, the miner boy, sings this song in The Princess and the Goblin by George Macdonald to scare away the creepy, night-time goblins who lurk around the mine.

Nonsense

I had a boat, and the boat had wings;
And I did dream that we went a flying
Over the heads of queens and kings,
Over the souls of dead and dying,
Up among the stars and the great white rings,
And where the Moon on her back is lying.

Mary Coleridge

Once

Once I was a monarch's daughter,
And sat on a lady's knee;
But am now a nightly rover,
Banished to the ivy tree.

Crying **hoo, hoo, hoo, hoo, hoo, hoo,**
Hoo, hoo, hoo, My feet are cold.

Pity me, for here you see me
Persecuted, poor, and old.

I once was a king's daughter
And sat on my father's knee
But now I'm a poor hoolet
And hide in a hollow tree

Anonymous

185

ALL THE DAY LONG

These delightful poems are all about the things we do in everyday life. We play with toys, feel happy, eat lunch, read books, kiss the people we love, and go to sleep – just as people have been doing for centuries.

Good Morning

The year's at the Spring,
And day's at the morn;
Morning's at seven;
The hillside's dew-pearled;
The lark's on the wing;
The snail's on the thorn;
God's in his heaven –
All's right with the world.

Robert Browning

Three Little Rules

Three little rules we all should keep.
To make life happy and bright.

Smile in the morning, smile at noon.
And keep on smiling at night.

Anonymous

Hair Brushing

One for a tangle,
One for a curl,
One for a boy
And one for a girl,
One to make a parting,
One to tie a bow,
One to blow the cobwebs out
And one to make it grow.

Anonymous

From Poem to her Daughter

Daughter, take this amulet,
tie it with cord and caring.
I'll make you a chain of coral and pearl
to glow on your neck. I'll dress you nobly.
A gold clasp too — fine, without flaw,
to keep with you always.
When you bathe, sprinkle perfume, and
    weave your hair in braids,
string jasmine for the counterpane.
Wear your clothes like a bride,
anklets for your feet, bracelets for your arms…
Don't forget rosewater,
don't forget henna for the palms of your hands…

Mwana Kupona binti Msham

Amulet a charm to keep
the wearer safe
Counterpane bedspread
Henna a reddish-brown dye

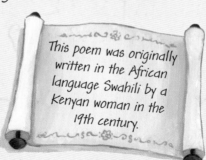

This poem was originally
written in the African
language Swahili by a
Kenyan woman in the
19th century.

A Kiss when I Wake

A kiss when I wake in the morning
A kiss when I go to bed,
A kiss when I burn my fingers,
A kiss when I bump my head.
A kiss when my bath begins
A kiss when my bath is over,
My mamma is as full of kisses
As nurse is full of pins.
A kiss when I play with my rattle;
A kiss when I pull her hair,
She covered me all over with kisses
The day that I fell down stair.
A kiss when I give her trouble,
A kiss when I give her joy;
There's nothing like mamma's kisses
To her own little baby boy.

Anonymous

The Hurt Hand

Pat it, kiss it,
Stroke it, bless it;
Three days' sunshine, three days' rain,
Little hand all well again.

Anonymous

Baby Mine

Baby mine, over the trees;
Baby mine, over the flowers;
Baby mine, over the sunshine;
Baby mine, over the showers;

Baby mine, over the land;
Baby mine, over the water.
Oh, when had a mother before
Such a sweet – such a sweet, little daughter!

Kate Greenaway

My Shadow

I have a little shadow that goes in and out with me,
And what can be the use of him is more than I can see.
He is very, very like me from the heels up to the head;
And I see him jump before me, when I jump into my bed.
The funniest thing about him is the way he likes to grow –
Not at all like proper children, which is always very slow;
For he sometimes shoots up taller like an india-rubber ball,
And he sometimes goes so little that there's none of
    him at all.

He hasn't got a notion of how children
    ought to play,
And can only make a fool of me in
    every sort of way.
He stays so close behind me, he's a
    coward you can see;

I'd think shame to stick to nursie as that shadow sticks to me!
One morning, very early, before the sun was up,
I rose and found the shining dew on every buttercup;
But my lazy little shadow, like an arrant sleepy-head,
Had stayed at home behind me and was fast asleep in bed.

Robert Louis Stevenson

Arrant
complete

Godfrey Gordon Gustavus Gore

Godfrey Gordon Gustavus Gore
Godfrey Gordon Gustavus Gore –
No doubt you have heard the name before –
Was a boy who never would shut a door!

The wind might whistle, the wind might roar,
And teeth be aching and throats be sore,
But still he never would shut the door.
His father would beg, his mother implore,
"Godfrey Gordon Gustavus Gore,
    We really do wish you would shut the door!"

Their hands they wrung, their hair they tore;
But Godfrey Gordon Gustavus Gore
Was deaf as the buoy out at the Nore.
When he walked forth the folks would roar,
"Godfrey Gordon Gustavus Gore,
    Why don't you think to shut the door?"

They rigged up a Shutter with sail and oar,
And threatened to pack off Gustavus Gore
On a voyage of penance to Singapore.

But he begged for mercy and said, "No more!
Pray do not send me to Singapore
On a Shutter, and then I will shut the door!"

"You will?" said his parents; "then keep on shore!
But mind you do! For the plague is sore
Of a fellow that never will shut the door,
Godfrey Gordon Gustavus Gore!"

William Brighty Rands

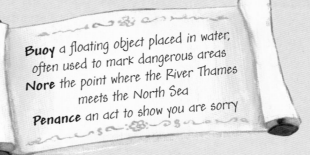

Buoy a floating object placed in water,
often used to mark dangerous areas
Nore the point where the River Thames
meets the North Sea
Penance an act to show you are sorry

From A Woman's Questions

How old is God? Has he grey hair?
Can He see yet? Where did He have to stay
Before – you know – he had made – Anywhere?
Who does He pray to – when He has to pray?

How many drops are in the sea?
How many stars? – Well, then, you ought to know
How many flowers are on an apple tree?
How does the wind look when it doesn't blow?

Where does the rainbow end? And why
Did – Captain Kidd – bury the gold there? When
Will this world burn? And will the firemen try
To put the fire out with the engines then?

If you should ever die, may we
Have pumpkins growing in the garden, so
My fairy godmother can come for me,
When there's a prince's ball, and let me go?

Sarah Morgan Bryan Piatt

The Dumb Soldier

When the grass was closely mown,
Walking on the lawn alone,
In the turf a hole I found,
And hid a soldier underground.

Spring and daisies came apace;
Grasses hide my hiding place;
Grasses run like a green sea
O'er the lawn up to my knee.

Under grass alone he lies,
Looking up with leaden eyes,
Scarlet coat and pointed gun,
To the stars and to the sun.

When the grass is ripe like grain,
When the scythe is stoned again,
When the lawn is shaven clear,
Then my hole shall reappear.

I shall find him, never fear,
I shall find my grenadier;
But for all that's gone and come,
I shall find my soldier dumb.

He has lived, a little thing,
In the grassy woods of spring;
Done, if he could tell me true,
Just as I should like to do.

Grenadier a type
of soldier

He has seen the starry hours
And the springing of the flowers;
And the fairy things that pass
In the forests of the grass.

In the silence he has heard
Talking bee and ladybird,
And the butterfly has flown
O'er him as he lay alone.

Not a word will he disclose,
Not a word of all he knows.
I must lay him on the shelf,
And make up the tale myself.

Robert Louis Stevenson

A Birthday Song

Our darling Roberta,
No sorrow shall hurt her
If we can prevent it
Her whole life long.
Her birthday's our fete day,
We'll make it our great day,
And give her our presents
And sing her our song.
May pleasures attend her
And may the Fates send her
The happiest journey
Along her life's way.
With skies bright above her
And dear ones to love her!
Dear Bob! Many happy
Returns of the day!

E Nesbit

In The Railway Children, Roberta's mother writes this song for the family to sing on her 12th birthday.

A Nursery Song

One cannot turn a minute,
But mischief there you're in it,
A-getting at my books, John,
With mighty bustling looks, John;
Or poking at the roses
In midst of which your nose is;
Or climbing on a table,
No matter how unstable,
And turning up your quaint eye
And half-shut teeth with 'Mayn't I?
Or else you're off at play, John,
Just as you'd be all day, John,
With hat or not, as happens,
And there you dance, and clap hands,
Or on the grass go rolling,
Or plucking flowers, or bowling,
And getting me expenses
With losing balls o'er fences;

And *see* what flow'rs the weather
Has render'd fit to gather;
And, when we home must jog, you
Shall ride my back, you rogue you.
Your hat adorn'd with fir-leaves,
Horse-chestnut, oak, and vine-leaves;
And so, with green o'erhead, John,
Shall whistle home to bed, John.
But *see*, the sun shines brightly;
Come, put your hat on rightly,
And we'll among the bushes,
And hear your friends the thrushes.

Leigh Hunt

205

The Teacher

I'd like to be a teacher, and have a clever brain,
Calling out,

"Attention, please!"
and

"Must I speak in vain?"

I'd be quite strict with boys and girls whose minds I had to train,
And all the books and maps and things I'd carefully explain;
I'd make then learn the dates of kings,
    and all the capes of Spain;
But I wouldn't be a teacher if...
    I couldn't use the cane.
      Would you?

C J Dennis

Quick, Quick

Quick, quick
The cat's been sick
Where, where?
Under the chair.
Hasten, hasten
Fetch a basin.
Too late, too late,
'Tis all in vain,
The cat has licked it
Up again.

Anonymous

The Story of Johnny Head-in-Air

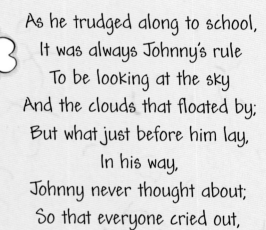

As he trudged along to school,
It was always Johnny's rule
To be looking at the sky
And the clouds that floated by;
But what just before him lay,
In his way,
Johnny never thought about;
So that everyone cried out,

**"Look at little Johnny there,
Little Johnny Head-in-Air!"**

Running just in Johnny's way
Came a little dog one day;
Johnny's eyes were still astray
Up on high,
In the sky;
And he never heard them cry

"Johnny, mind, the dog is nigh!"
Bump!
Dump!

Down they fell, with such a thump,
Dog and Johnny in a lump!

Once, with head as high as ever,
Johnny walked beside the river.
Johnny watched the swallows trying
Which was cleverest at flying.
Oh! What fun!
Johnny watched the bright round sun
Going in and coming out;

This was all he thought about.
So he strode on, only think!
To the river's very brink,
Where the bank was and steep,
And the water very deep;
And the fishes, in a row,
Stared to see him coming so.

One step more! Oh! Sad to tell!
Headlong in poor Johnny fell.
And the fishes, in dismay,
Wagged their tails and swam away.
There lay Johnny on his face,
With his nice red writing-case;
But, as they were passing by,
Two strong men had heard him cry;
And, with sticks, these two strong men
Hooked poor Johnny out again.

Oh! You should have seen him shiver
When they pulled him from the river.
He was in a sorry plight,

Dripping wet, and such a fright!
Wet all over, everywhere,
Clothes, and arms, and face, and hair:
Johnny never will forget
What it is to be so wet.

And the fishes, one, two, three,
Are come back again, you see;
Up they came the moment after,
To enjoy the fun and laughter.
Each popped out his little head,
And, to tease poor Johnny, said

**"Silly little Johnny, look,
You have lost your writing-book!"**

Heinrich Hoffmann

From A Boy's Aspirations

I was four yesterday – when I'm quite old,
I'll have a cricket-ball made of pure gold;
I'll carve the roast meat, and help soup and fish;
I'll get my feet wet whenever I wish;

I'll spend a hundred pounds every day;
I'll have the alphabet quite done away;
I'll have a parrot without a sharp beak;
I'll see a pantomime six times a week;

I'll have a rose-tree, always in bloom;
I'll keep a dancing bear in Mamma's room;
I'll spoil my best clothes, and not care a pin;
I'll have no visitors ever let in;

I'll never stand up to show that I'm grown;
No one shall say to me, "Don't throw a stone!"
I'll drop my butter'd toast on the new chintz;
I'll have no governess giving her hints.

I'll have a nursery up in the stars;
I'll lean through windows without any bars;
I'll sail without my nurse in a big boat;
I'll have no comforters tied round my throat;

I'll have a language with not a word spell'd;
I'll ride on horseback without being held;
I'll hear Mamma say, "My boy, good as gold!"
When I'm a grown-up man sixty years old.

Menella Bute Smedley

A Boy's Song

Where the pools are bright and deep,
Where the grey trout lies asleep,
Up the river and over the lea,
That's the way for Billy and me.

Where the blackbird sings the latest,
Where the hawthorn blooms the
    sweetest,
Where the nestlings chirp and flee,
That's the way for Billy and me.

Where the mowers mow the cleanest,
Where the hay lies thick and greenest,
There to track the homeward bee,
That's the way for Billy and me.

Lea meadow

Where the hazel bank is steepest,
Where the shadow falls the deepest,
Where the clustering nuts fall free,
That's the way for Billy and me.

Why the boys should drive away
Little sweet maidens from their play,
Or love to banter and fight so well,
That's the thing I never could tell.

But this I know, I love to play
Through the meadow, among the hay;
Up the water and over the lea,
That's the way for Billy and me.

James Hogg

My Books

I love my books
They are the homes
of queens and fairies,
Knights and gnomes.

Each time I read I make a call
On some quaint person large or small,
Who welcomes me with hearty hand
And leads me through his wonderland.

Each book is like
A city street
Along whose winding way I meet
New friends and old who laugh and sing
And take me off adventuring!

Anonymous

A Little Song of Life

Glad that I live am I;
That the sky is blue;
Glad for the country lanes,
And the fall of dew.

After the sun the rain;
After the rain the sun;
This is the way of life,
Till the work be done.

All that we need to do,
Be we low or high,
Is to see that we grow
Nearer the sky.

Lizette Woodworth Reese

Rose and the Lily

Rose dreamed she was a lily,
Lily dreamed she was a rose;
Robin dreamed he was a sparrow;
What the owl dreamed no one knows.

But they all woke up together
As happy as could be.
Said each: "You're lovely, neighbour,
But I'm very glad I'm me."

Anonymous

Jelly

Jelly on the plate
Jelly on the plate

Wibble wobble
Wibble wobble

Jelly on the plate

Anonymous

The Camel's Hump

The camel's hump is an ugly lump
Which well you may see at the Zoo;
But uglier yet is the hump we get
From having too little to do.

Kiddies and grown-ups too-oo-oo,
If we haven't enough to do-oo-oo,
We get the hump

Cameelious hump

The hump that is black and blue

We climb out of bed with a frouzly head
And a snarly-yarly voice;
We shiver and scowl, and we grunt and we growl
At our bath and our boots and our toys;

And there ought to be a corner for me
(And I know there is one for you)
When we get the hump

Cameelious hump

The hump that is black and blue!

The cure for this ill is not to sit still,
Or frowst with a book by the fire;
But to take a large hoe and a shovel also,
And dig till you gently perspire;

And then you will find that the sun and the wind,
And the Djinn of the Garden too,
Have lifted the hump
The horrible hump
The hump that is black and blue

I get it as well as you-oo-oo
If I haven't enough to do-oo-oo,
We all get the hump

Cameelious hump

Kiddies and grown-ups too!

Rudyard Kipling

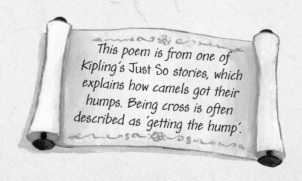

This poem is from one of Kipling's Just So stories, which explains how camels got their humps. Being cross is often described as 'getting the hump'.

Apples

An apple a day
Sends the doctor away
Apple in the morning
Doctor's warning
Roast apple at night
Starves the doctor outright
Eat an apple going to bed
Knock the doctor on the head

Anonymous

At the Zoo

First I saw the white bear, then I saw the black;
Then I saw the camel with a hump upon his back;
Then I saw the grey wolf, with mutton in his maw;
Then I saw the wombat waddle in the straw;
Then I saw the elephant a-waving of his trunk;
Then I saw the monkeys — mercy, how
unpleasantly they—smelt!

William Makepeace Thackeray

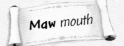

Maw *mouth*

The Use and Abuse of Toads

As into the garden Elizabeth ran
Pursued by the just indignation of Ann,
She trod on an object that lay in her road,
She trod on an object that looked like a toad.
It looked like a toad, and it looked so because
A toad was the actual object it was;
And after supporting Elizabeth's tread
It looked like a toad that was visibly dead.
Elizabeth, leaving her footprint behind,
Continued her flight on the wings of the wind,
And Ann in her anger was heard to arrive
At the toad that was not any longer alive.

She was heard to arrive, for the firmament rang
With the sound of a scream and the noise of a bang,
As her breath on the breezes she broadly bestowed
And fainted away on Elizabeth's toad.
Elizabeth, saved by the sole of her boot,
Escaped her insensible sister's pursuit;
And if ever hereafter she irritates Ann,
She will tread on a toad if she possibly can.

A E Housman

Firmament sky
Insensible unconscious

Dog Problems

Our dog Fred
Et the bread.

Our dog Dash
Et the hash.

Our dog Pete
Et the meat.

Our dog Davy
Et the gravy.

Our dog Toffee
Et the coffee.

Our dog Jake
Et the cake.

Our dog Trip
Et the dip.

And – the worst,
From the first, –

Our dog Fido
Et the pie-dough.

James Whitcomb Riley

The Story of Fidgety Philip

Let me see if Philip can
Be a little gentleman
Let me see, if he is able
To sit still for once at table:
Thus Papa bade Phil behave;
And Mamma look'd very grave.
But fidgety Phil,
He won't sit still;
He wriggles
and giggles,
And then, I declare
Swings backwards and forwards
And tilts up his chair,
Just like any rocking horse –
"Philip! I am getting cross!"

See the naughty restless child
Growing still more rude and wild.
Till his chair falls over quite.
Philip screams with all his might.

Catches at the cloth, but then
That makes matters worse again.
Down upon the ground they fall.
Glasses, plates, knives, forks and all.

How Mamma did fret and frown.
When she saw them tumbling down!
And Papa made such a face!
Philip is in sad disgrace.

Where is Philip, where is he?
Fairly cover'd up you see!
Cloth and all are lying on him;
He has pull'd down all upon him.
What a terrible to-do!
Dishes, glasses, snapt in two!
Here a knife, and there a fork!
Philip, this is cruel work.
Table all so bare, and ah!
Poor Papa, and poor Mamma
Look quite cross, and wonder how
They shall make their dinner now.

Heinrich Hoffmann

A Gustatory Achievement

Last Thanksgivin'-dinner we
Et at Granny's house, an' she
Had – ist like she alluz does –
Most an' best pies ever wuz.

Canned black burry-pie an' goose
Burry, squshin'-full o' juice;
An' rozburry – yes, an' plum –
Yes, an' churry-pie – um-yum!

Peach an' punkin, too, you bet.
Lawzy! I kin taste 'em yet!
Yes, an' custard-pie, an' mince!

An' – I – ain't – et – no –
pie – since!

James Whitcomb Riley

The person in this poem is remembering a Thanksgiving dinner, the feast Americans celebrate in November.

Little Things

Little drops of water,
Little grains of sand,
Make the mighty ocean
And the pleasant land.
Little deeds of kindness,
Little words of love,
Make our world an Eden
Like the Heaven above.

Julia Carney

Arabella Miller

Little Arabella Miller
Had a fuzzy caterpillar.
First it climbed upon her mother,
Then upon her baby brother.
They said, "Arabella Miller,
Put away your caterpillar!"

Anonymous

My Treasures

These nuts, that I keep in the back of the nest,
Where all my tin soldiers are lying at rest,
Were gathered in Autumn by nursie and me
In a wood with a well by the side of the sea.

This whistle we made and how clearly it sounds!
By the side of a field at the end of the grounds.
Of a branch of a plane, with a knife of
  my own,
It was nursie who made it,
  and nursie alone!

The stone, with the white and the yellow and grey,
We discovered I cannot tell HOW far away;
And I carried it back although weary and cold,
For though father denies it, I'm sure it is gold.

But of all my treasures the last is the king,
For there's very few children possess such a thing;
And that is a chisel, both handle and blade,
Which a man who was really a
carpenter made.

Robert Louis Stevenson

The Worm

No, little worm, you need not slip
Into your hole, with such a skip;
Drawing the gravel as you glide
On to your smooth and slimy side.
I'm not a crow, poor worm, not I,
Peeping about your holes to spy,
And fly away with you in air,
To give my young ones each a share.

No, and I'm not a rolling-stone,
Creaking along with hollow groan;
Nor am I of the naughty crew,
Who don't care what poor worms go through,
But trample on them as they lie,
Rather than pass them gently by;
Or keep them dangling on a hook,
Choked in a dismal pond or brook,
Till some poor fish comes swimming past,
And finishes their pain at last.

For my part, I could never bear
Your tender flesh to hack and tear,
  Forgetting that poor worms endure
    As much as I should, to be sure,
      If any giant should come and jump
      On to my back, and kill me plump,
      Or run my heart through with a scythe,
    And think it fun to see me writhe!
  O no, I'm only looking about,
To see you wriggle in and out,
And drawing together your slimy rings,
Instead of feet, like other things:
So, little worm, don't slide and slip
Into your hole, with such a skip.

Ann Taylor

Peek-a-Boo

The cunningest thing that a baby can do
Is the very first time it plays peek-a-boo;

When it hides its pink little face in its hands,
And crows, and shows that it understands

What nurse, and mamma and papa, too,
Mean when they hide and cry,

"peek-a-boo, peek-a-boo."

Oh, what a wonderful thing it is,
When they find that baby can play like this;

And everyone listens, and thinks it true
That baby's gurgle means

"peek-a-boo, peek-a-boo."

And over and over the changes are rung
On the marvellous infant who talks so young.

I wonder if anyone ever knew
A baby that never played

"peek-a-boo, peek-a-boo."

'Tis old as the hills are. I believe
Cain was taught it by Mother Eve;

For Cain was an innocent baby, too,
And I am sure he played

"Peek-a-boo, peek-a-boo."

And the whole world full of the children of men,
Have all of them played that game since then.

Kings and princes and beggars, too,
Everyone has played

"Peek-a-boo, peek-a-boo."

Thief and robber and ruffian bold,
The crazy tramp and the drunkard old,

All have been babies who laughed and knew
How to hide, and play

"Peek-a-boo, peek-a-boo."

Ella Wheeler Wilcox

Wash the Dishes

Wash the dishes,
Wipe the dishes,
Ring the bell for tea.

Three good wishes,
Three good kisses,
I will give to thee.

Anonymous

Coffee and Tea

Molly my sister and I fell out,
And what do you think it was all about?
She loved coffee and I loved tea,
And that was the reason we couldn't agree!

Anonymous

My Kingdom

Down by a shining water well
I found a very little dell,
No higher than my head.
The heather and the gorse about
In summer bloom were coming out,
Some yellow and some red.

I called the little pool a sea;
The little hills were big to me;
For I am very small.
I made a boat, I made a town,
I searched the caverns up and down,
And named them one and all.

And all about was mine, I said,
The little sparrows overhead,
The little minnows too.
This was the world and I was king;
For me the bees came by to sing,

For me the swallows flew.
I played there were no deeper seas,
Nor any wider plains than these,
Nor other kings than me.
At last I heard my mother call
Out from the house at evenfall,
To call me home to tea.

And I must rise and leave my dell,
And leave my dimpled water well,
And leave my heather blooms.
Alas! And as my home I neared,
How very big my nurse appeared.
How great and cool the rooms!

Robert Louis Stevenson

From # Night

The sun descending in the west,
The evening star does shine;
The birds are silent in their nest,
And I must seek for mine.
The moon like a flower,
In heaven's high bower,
With silent delight
Sits and smiles on the night.

William Blake

Little Fishes in a Brook

Little fishes in a brook,
Father caught them on a hook,
Mother fried them in a pan,
Johnnie eats them like a man.

Anonymous

The Lost Doll

I once had a sweet little doll, dears,
The prettiest doll in the world;
Her cheeks were so red and white, dears,
And her hair was so charmingly curled.
But I lost my poor little doll, dears,
As I played on the heath one day;
And I cried for her more than a week, dears,
But I never could find where she lay.

I found my poor little doll, dears,
As I played on the heath one day;
Folks say she is terribly changed, dears,
For her paint is all washed away,
And her arms trodden off by the cows, dears,
And her hair not the least bit curled;
Yet for old sake's sake, she is still, dears,
The prettiest doll in the world.

Charles Kingsley

The Unseen Playmate

When children are playing alone on the green,
In comes the playmate that never was seen.
When children are happy and lonely and good,
The Friend of the Children comes out of the wood.

Nobody heard him, and nobody saw,
His is a picture you never could draw,
But he's sure to be present, abroad or at home,
When children are happy and playing alone.

He lies in the laurels, he runs on the grass,
He sings when you tinkle the musical glass;
Whene'er you are happy and cannot tell why,
The Friend of the Children is sure to be by!

He loves to be little, he hates to be big,
'Tis he that inhabits the caves that you dig;
'Tis he when you play with your soldiers of tin
That sides with the Frenchmen and never can win.

'Tis he, when at night you go off to your bed,
Bids you go to sleep and not trouble your head;
For wherever they're lying, in cupboard or shelf,
'Tis he will take care of your playthings himself!

Robert Louis Stevenson

A Good Play

We built a ship upon the stairs
All made of the back-bedroom chairs,
And filled it full of sofa pillows
To go a-sailing on the billows.

We took a saw and several nails,
And water in the nursery pails;
And Tom said, "Let us also take
An apple and a slice of cake;"
Which was enough for Tom and me
To go a-sailing on, till tea.

We sailed along for
   days and days,
And had the very best
   of plays;
But Tom fell out and
   hurt his knee,
So there was no one
   left but me.

Robert Louis Stevenson

At the Seaside

When I was down beside the sea
A wooden spade they gave to me
To dig the sandy shore.
My holes were empty like a cup.
In every hole the sea came up,
Till it could come no more.

Robert Louis Stevenson

The Children's Hour

Between the dark and the daylight,
    When the night is beginning to lower,
Comes a pause in the day's occupations,
    That is known as the Children's Hour.

I hear in the chamber above me
    The patter of little feet,
The sound of a door that is opened,
    And voices soft and sweet.

From my study I see in the lamplight,
    Descending the broad hall stair,
Grave Alice, and laughing Allegra,
    And Edith with golden hair.

A whisper, and then a silence:
    Yet I know by their merry eyes
They are plotting and planning together
    To take me by surprise.

A sudden rush from the stairway,
    A sudden raid from the hall!
By three doors left unguarded
    They enter my castle wall!

They climb up into my turret
    O'er the arms and back of my chair;
If I try to escape, they surround me;
    They seem to be everywhere.

They almost devour me with kisses,
   Their arms about me entwine,
Till I think of the Bishop of Bingen
   In his Mouse-Tower on the Rhine!

Do you think, O blue-eyed banditti,
   Because you have scaled the wall,
Such an old mustache as I am
   Is not a match for you all!

I have you fast in my fortress,
    And will not let you depart,
But put you down into the dungeon
    In the round–tower of my heart.

And there will I keep you forever,
    Yes, forever and a day,
Till the walls shall crumble to ruin,
    And moulder in dust away!

Henry Wadsworth Longfellow

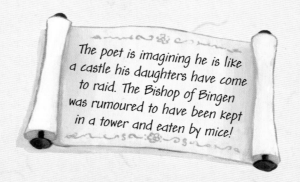

The poet is imagining he is like a castle his daughters have come to raid. The Bishop of Bingen was rumoured to have been kept in a tower and eaten by mice!

The Land of Story Books

At evening when the lamp is lit,
Around the fire my parents sit;
They sit at home and talk and sing,
And do not play at anything.

Now, with my little gun, I crawl
All in the dark along the wall,
And follow round the forest track
Away behind the sofa back.

There, in the night, where none can spy,
All in my hunter's camp I lie,
And play at books that I have read
Till it is time to go to bed.

These are the hills, these are the woods,
These are my starry solitudes;
And there the river by whose brink
The roaring lions come to drink.

I see the others far away
As if in firelit camp they lay,
And I, like to an Indian scout,
Around their party prowled about.

So, when my nurse comes in for me,
Home I return across the sea,
And go to bed with backward looks
At my dear land of story books.

Robert Louis Stevenson

Imagine a dark room lit only by a lamp. Behind the furniture would be a perfect place to pretend to be a hunter or explorer.

Z Z Z Z Z Z

A Good Boy

I woke before the morning, I was happy all the day,
I never said an ugly word, but smiled and stuck to play.

And now at last the sun is going down behind the wood,
And I am very happy, for I know that I've been good.

My bed is waiting cool and fresh, with linen smooth and fair,
And I must be off to sleepsin-by, and not forget my prayer.

I know that, till tomorrow I shall see the sun arise,
No ugly dream shall fright my mind, no ugly sight my eyes.

But slumber hold me tightly till I waken in the dawn,
And hear the thrushes singing in the lilacs round the lawn.

Robert Louis Stevenson

Tumbling

In jumping and tumbling
We spend the whole day,
Till night by arriving
Has finished our play.
What then? One and all,
There's no more to be said,
As we tumbled all day,
So we tumble to bed.

Anonymous

Brother and Sister

"Sister, sister, go to bed!
Go and rest your weary head."
Thus the prudent brother said.

"Do you want a battered hide,
Or scratches to your face applied?"
Thus his sister calm replied.

"Sister, do not raise my wrath.
I'd make you into mutton broth
As easily as kill a moth"

The sister raised her beaming eye
And looked on him indignantly
And sternly answered, "Only try!"

Off to the cook he quickly ran.
"Dear Cook, please lend a frying pan
To me as quickly as you can."

"And wherefore should I lend it you?"
"The reason, Cook, is plain to view.
I wish to make an Irish stew."

"What meat is in that stew to go?"
"My sister'll be the contents!"
   "Oh"
"You'll lend the pan to me, Cook?"
   "No!"

Moral: Never stew your sister.

Lewis Carroll

The Ferry of Shadowtown

Sway to and fro in the twilight grey;
This is the ferry for Shadowtown;
It always sails at the end of
the day,
Just as the darkness
closes down.

Rest, little head, on my shoulder so
A sleepy kiss is the only fare;
Drifting away from the world we go,
Baby and I in the rocking chair.

See, where the fire logs glow and spark,
Glitter the lights of the shadowland;
The raining drops on the window, hark!
Are ripples lapping upon its strand.

There, where the mirror is glancing dim,
A lake lies shimmering, cool and still;
Blossoms are waving above its brim,
Those over there on the window sill.

Rock slow, more slow, in the dusky light,
Silently lower the anchor down,
Dear little passenger, say "Good night!"
We've reached the harbour for Shadowtown!

Ethelbert Nevin

The Lamplighter

My tea is nearly ready and the sun has left the sky.
It's time to take the window to see Leerie going by;
For every night at teatime and before you take your seat,
With lantern and with ladder he comes posting up the street.

Now Tom would be a driver and Maria go to sea,
And my papa's a banker and as rich as he can be;
But I, when I am stronger and can choose what
    I'm to do,
O Leerie, I'll go round at night and light the
    lamps with you!

For we are very lucky, with a lamp before the door,
And Leerie stops to light it as he lights so many more;
And oh! before you hurry by with ladder
    and with light;
O Leerie, see a little child and nod to
    him tonight!

Robert Louis Stevenson

Street lamps used to be lit by gas, and a lamplighter had to light each one.

I See the Moon

I see the moon,
And the moon sees me.
God bless the moon,
And God bless me!

Anonymous

Goodnight Sleep Tight

Goodnight, sleep tight,
Hope the bugs don't bite!
Wake up bright in the morning light.
To do what's right with all your might.

Anonymous

Bedtime in Summer

In winter I get up at night
And dress by yellow candle-light.
In summer quite the other way,
I have to go to bed by day.
I have to go to bed and see
The birds still hopping on the tree,
Or hear the grown-up people's feet
Still going past me in the street.
And does it not seem hard to you,
When all the sky is clear and blue,
And I should like so much to play,
To have to go to bed by day?

Robert Louis Stevenson

Young Night-thought

All night long and every night,
When my mama puts out the light,
I see the people marching by,
As plain as day before my eye.
Armies and emperor and kings,
All carrying different kinds of things,
And marching in so grand a way,
You never saw the like by day.
So fine a show was never seen
At the great circus on the green;
For every kind of beast and man
Is marching in that caravan.
As first they move a little slow,
But still the faster on they go,
And still beside me close I keep
Until we reach the town of Sleep.

Robert Louis Stevenson

Escape at Bedtime

The lights from the parlour and kitchen shone out
Through the blinds and the windows and bars;
And high overhead and all moving about,
There were thousands of millions of stars.
There ne'er were such thousands of leaves on a tree,
Nor of people in church or the Park,
As the crowds of the stars that looked down upon me,
And that glittered and winked in the dark.

The Dog, and the Plough, and the Hunter, and all,
And the star of the sailor, and Mars,
These shown in the sky, and the pail by the wall
Would be half full of water and stars.
They saw me at last, and they chased me with cries,
And they soon had me packed into bed;
But the glory kept shining and bright in my eyes,
And the stars going round in my head.

Robert Louis Stevenson

The Dog, the Plough and the Hunter are patterns of stars in the sky, called constellations.

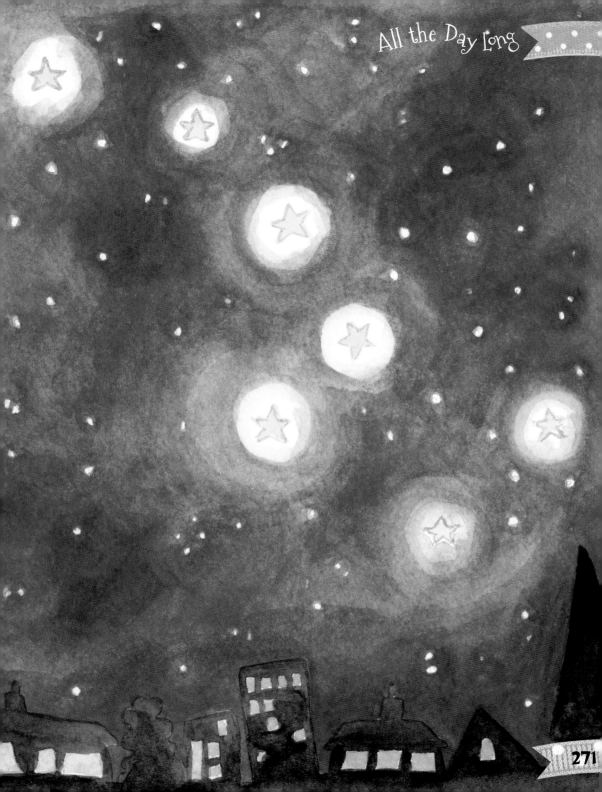

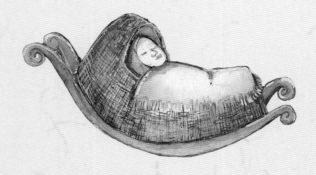

Dreams

Here we are all, by day; by night we're hurl'd
By dreams, each one into a several world.

Robert Herrick

Several *separate*

The Moon

The moon has a face like the clock in the hall;
She shines on thieves on the garden wall,
On streets and fields and harbour quays,
And birdies asleep in the forks of the trees.
The squalling cat and the squeaking mouse,
The howling dog by the door of the house,
The bat that lies in bed at noon,
All love to be out by the light of the moon.
But all of the things that belong to the day
Cuddle to sleep to be out of her way;
And flowers and children close their eyes
Till up in the morning the sun shall arise.

Robert Louis Stevenson

My Bed is a Boat

My bed is like a little boat;
Nurse helps me in when I embark;
She girds me in my sailor's coat
And starts me in the dark.
At night I go on board and say
Goodnight to all my friends on shore;
I shut my eyes and sail away
And see and hear no more.
And sometimes things to bed I take,
As prudent sailors have to do;
Perhaps a slice of wedding-cake,
Perhaps a toy or two.
All night across the dark we steer;
But when the day returns at last,
Safe in my room beside the pier,
I find my vessel fast.

Robert Louis Stevenson

Gird to wrap up

274

The Falling Star

I saw a star slide down the sky,
Blind the north as it went by,
Too burning and too quick to hold,
Too lovely to be bought or sold,
Good only to make wishes on
And then forever to be gone.

Sara Teasdale

All Through the Night

Sleep my love and peace attend thee,
All through the night;
Guardian angels, God will send thee,
All through the night.
Soft the drowsy hours are creeping,
Hill and vale in slumber sleeping,
Love alone His watch is keeping,
All through the night.
While the moon her watch is keeping,
All through the night;
While the weary world is sleeping,
All through the night.
O'er the spirit gently stealing,
Visions of delight revealing,
Breathes a pure and holy feeling,
All through the night.

Alfred, Lord Tennyson

A Cradle Song

The angels are stooping
Above your bed;
They weary of trooping
With the whimpering dead.
God's laughing in Heaven
To see you so good;
The Sailing Seven
Are gay with His mood.
I sigh that kiss you,
For I must own
That I shall miss you
When you have grown.

W B Yeats

The Sailing Seven
are a cluster of
stars in the sky.

277

Planning

In summer when I go to bed,
The sun still streaming overhead,
My bed becomes so small and hot
With sheets and pillow in a knot,
And then I lie and try to see
The things I'd really like to be.

I think I'd be a glossy cat,
A little plump, but not too fat.
I'd never touch a bird or mouse,
I'm much too busy round the house.

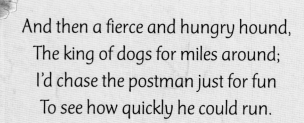

And then a fierce and hungry hound,
The king of dogs for miles around;
I'd chase the postman just for fun
To see how quickly he could run.

Perhaps I'd be a crocodile
Within the marshes of the Nile,
And paddle in the river-bed
With dripping mud-caps on my head.

Or maybe next a mountain goat
With shaggy whiskers at my throat,
Leaping streams and jumping rocks
In stripey pink and purple socks.

Or else I'd be a polar bear
And on an iceberg make my lair;
I'd keep a shop in Baffin Sound
To sell icebergs by the pound.

And then I'd be a wise old frog
Squatting on a sunken log,
I'd teach the fishes lots of games
And how to read and write their names.

An Indian lion then I'd be
And lounge about on my settee;
I'd feed on nothing but bananas
And spend all day in my pyjamas.

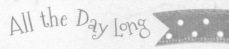

I'd like to be a tall giraffe,
Making lots of people laugh,
I'd do a tap dance in the street
With little bells upon my feet.

And then I'd be a foxy fox
Streaking through the hollyhocks,
Horse or hound would ne'er catch me;
I'm a master of disguise, you see.

I think I'd be a chimpanzee
With musical ability,
I'd play a silver clarinet
Or form a Monkey String Quartet.

And then a snake with scales of gold
Guarding hoards of wealth untold,
No thief would dare to steal a pin –
But friends of mine I would let in.

But then before I really know
Just what I'd be or where I'd go,
My bed becomes so wide and deep
And all my thoughts are fast asleep.

Thomas Hood

A WONDERFUL WORLD

Read charming verses about trees,
flowers, animals, the weather,
the seasons and the sea. These poems
celebrate the wonderful world we live in
and remind us that nature is special,
beautiful and exciting.

Caterpillar

Brown and furry
Caterpillar in a hurry,
Take your walk
To the shady leaf, or stalk,
Or what not,
Which may be the chosen spot.
No toad spy you,
Hovering bird of prey pass by you;
Spin and die,
To live again a butterfly.

Christina Rossetti

Butterfly

What is a butterfly? At best
He's but a caterpillar dressed.

Benjamin Franklin

Hurt no Living Thing

Hurt no living thing:
Ladybird, nor butterfly,
Nor moth with dusty wing,
Nor cricket chirping cheerily,
Nor grasshopper so light of leap,
Nor dancing gnat, nor beetle fat,
Nor harmless worms that creep.

Christina Rossetti

White Sheep

White sheep, white sheep,
On a blue hill,
When the wind stops
You all stand still.

When the wind blows,
You walk away slow.
White sheep, white sheep,
Where do you go?

Anonymous

This could be a poem about sheep, but it might also be about the sky and clouds.

February Twilight

I stood beside a hill
Smooth with new-laid snow,
A single star looked out
From the cold evening glow.
There was no other creature
That saw what I could see –
I stood and watched the evening star
As long as it watched me.

Sara Teasdale

Tweet tweet! tweet tweet!

From Strange Meetings

The stars must make an awful noise
In whirling round the sky;
Yet somehow I can't even hear
Their loudest song or sigh.

So it is wonderful to think
One blackbird can outsing
The voice of all the swarming stars
On any day in Spring.

Harold Monro

Baby Seed Song

Little brown seed, oh! little brown brother,
Are you awake in the dark?
Here we lie cosily, close to each other:
Hark to the song of the lark—

    "Waken!" the lark says, "waken
       and dress you,
      Put on your green coats and gay,
      Blue sky will shine on you, sunshine
      caress you—
    Waken! 'tis morning—'tis May!"

  Little brown brother, oh! little brown brother,
What kind of flower will you be?
I'll be a poppy—all white, like my mother;
 Do be a poppy like me.
  What! You're a sunflower? How I shall miss you
 When you're grown golden and high!
But I shall send all the bees up to kiss you;
Little brown brother, goodbye!

E Nesbit

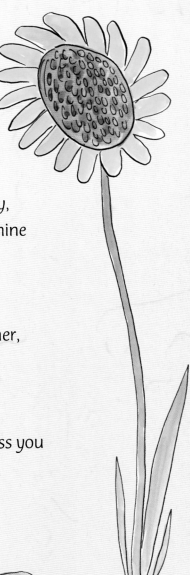

All the Year Round

January brings the snow,
makes our feet and fingers glow.

February brings the rain,
Thaws the frozen lake again.

March brings breezes loud and shrill,
stirs the dancing daffodil.

April brings the primrose sweet,
Scatters daises at our feet.

May brings flocks of pretty lambs,
Skipping by their fleecy dams.

June brings tulips, lilies, roses,
Fills the children's hands with posies.

Hot **July** brings cooling showers,
Apricots and gillyflowers.

August brings the sheaves of corn,
Then the harvest home is borne.

Warm **September** brings the fruit,
Sportsmen then begin to shoot.

Fresh **October** brings the pheasants,
Then to gather nuts is pleasant.

Dull **November** brings the blast,
Then the leaves are whirling fast.

Chill **December** brings the sleet,
Blazing fire, and Christmas treat.

Sara Coleridge

Gillyflowers
carnations

Seal Lullaby

Oh! Hush thee, my baby, the night is behind us,
And black are the waters that sparkled so green.
The moon, o'er the combers, looks downward to find us
At rest in the hollows that rustle between.
Where billow meets billow, there soft be thy pillow;
Ah, weary wee flipperling, curl at thy ease!
The storm shall not wake thee, nor shark overtake thee,
Asleep in the arms of the slow-swinging seas.

Rudyard Kipling

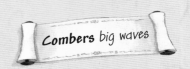

Combers big waves

Seals sleep floating just under the water and can come up to breathe without waking up.

From Wild Swans at Coole

The trees are in their autumn beauty,
The woodland paths are dry,
Under the October twilight the water
Mirrors a still sky;
Upon the brimming water among the stones
Are nine-and-fifty Swans.

W B Yeats

Swan

Swan swam over the sea;
Swim, swan, swim.
Swan swam back again;
Well swum swan.

Anonymous

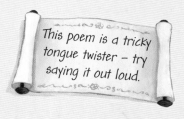

This poem is a tricky
tongue twister – try
saying it out loud.

The Ant

My child, observe the useful Ant,
How hard she works each day.
She works as hard as adamant
(That's very hard, they say).
She has no time to gallivant;
She has no time to play.
Let Fido chase his tail all day;
Let Kitty play at tag:
She has no time to throw away,
She has no tail to wag.
She scurries round from morn till night;
She never, never sleeps;
She seizes everything in sight,
And drags it home with all her might,
And all she takes she keeps.

Oliver Herford

A Lark

Lark-bird, lark-bird, soaring high,
Are you never weary?
When you reach the empty sky
Are the clouds not dreary?
Don't you sometimes long to be
A silent goldfish in the sea?

Goldfish, goldfish, diving deep,
Are you never sad, say?
When you feel the cold waves creep
Are you really glad, say?
Don't you sometimes long to sing
And be a lark-bird on the wing?

Lawrence Alma-Tadema

My Heart's in the Highlands

My heart's in the Highlands, my heart is not here;
My heart's in the Highlands a-chasing the deer;
Chasing the wild deer, and following the roe,
My heart's in the Highlands wherever I go.
Farewell to the Highlands, farewell to the North,
The birthplace of valour, the country of worth;
Wherever I wander, wherever I rove,
The hills of the Highlands for ever I love.

The Highlands are a beautiful, mountainous region in the far north of Scotland. In this poem, the speaker is remembering the place he loves but has had to leave.

Farewell to the mountains high covered with snow;
Farewell to the straths and green valleys below;
Farewell to the forests and wild hanging woods;
Farewell to the torrents and loud-pouring floods.
My heart's in the Highlands, my heart is not here,
My heart's in the Highlands a-chasing the deer;
Chasing the wild deer, and following the roe,
My heart's in the Highlands wherever I go.

Robert Burns

Strath a broad valley

Buttercup

A Flower Alphabet

A for the Aconite, first of the year,
  With its pretty green ruff and its message of cheer.

B for the Buttercup, able to hold
  Dewdrop and rain in its chalice of gold.

C for the Cowslip, sweet joy of the spring;
  When cowslips are blooming the nightingales sing.

D for the Daisy, white star of the grass,
  Lifting its bright eye to us as we pass.

E for the Eglantine, lovely wild rose,
  Sheds fragrance of sweetbriar wherever it grows.

F for the Foxglove, the sentinel tall,
  Guarding the forest from summer to fall.

G for the Gorse of rich golden delight;
  Linnaeus went down on his knees at the sight.

Eglantine

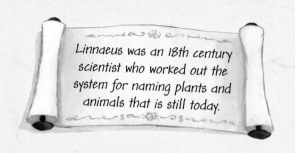

Linnaeus was an 18th century scientist who worked out the system for naming plants and animals that is still today.

Iris

H for the Harebell, so fragile, yet strong
   The dear little Bluebells of Scotland in song.

I for the Iris which grows by the stream,
   The flower of the Rainbow, how golden its gleam!

J for St John's Wort, of medical fame,
   Balm of the Warrior's Wound was its name.

K for the Kingcup that loves marshy fields,
   And glorious the harvest of gold that it yields!

L for the Ling, the dear flower of the heath,
   How tender its colour, how fragrant its breath!

M for the Meadowsweet, pleasant and rare
   Is the perfume with which it enchanteth the air!

Ling another name for heather

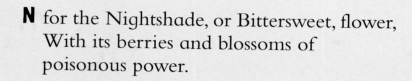
Nightshade

N for the Nightshade, or Bittersweet, flower,
With its berries and blossoms of
poisonous power.

O for the Oxlip, a flower that you'll find
When cowslips and orchids in posies you bind.

P for the Primrose, recalling to sight
Paths in the woodlands a-shimmer with light.

Q for the Quaking grass, name that it takes
From the way it unceasingly shivers and shakes.

R for the Rest-harrow, staying the plough,
Food for the gentle-eyed, ruminant cow.

S for the Speedwell, of tenderest blue;
From the skies it has taken its exquisite hue.

Speedwell

T for the Traveller's Joy that you'll find
Where sweet, sheltering hedgerows wander and wind.

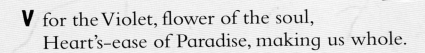

Windflower

U for the Upright Sea-lavender flower;
The sand-swallows claim it for
sheltering bower.

V for the Violet, flower of the soul,
Heart's-ease of Paradise, making us whole.

W for Windflower, so fair to the sight,
That throws o'er the woodlands her mantle
of light.

X forms a cross in the Passion-flower wild
In Southern America, balmy and mild.

Y for the Yarrow, all wayfarers know,
As it grows by the wayside wherever you go.

Z is the ribbon this posy to bind,
With the thoughts and the fragrance it brings
to your mind.

Anonymous

The Cat of Cats

I am the cat of cats. I am
The everlasting cat!
Cunning, and old, and sleek as jam,
The everlasting cat!
I hunt vermin in the night —
The everlasting cat!
For I see best without the light —
The everlasting cat!

William Brighty Rands

Over in the Meadow

Over in the meadow,
In the sand in the sun,
Lived an old mother toadie,
And her little toadie one,
"Wink!" said the mother;
"I wink!" said the one,
So they winked and they blinked,
In the sand in the sun.

Over in the meadow,
Where the stream runs blue,
Lived an old mother fish,
And her little fishes two,
"Swim!" said the mother;
"We swim!" said the two,
So they swam and they leaped,
Where the stream runs blue.

Over in the meadow,
In a hole in a tree,
Lived an old mother bluebird,
And her little birdies three,
"**Sing!**" said the mother;
"We sing!" said the three,
So they sang and were glad,
In a hole in the tree.

Over in the meadow,
In the reeds on the shore,
Lived an old mother muskrat,
And her little ratties four,
"**Dive!**" said the mother;
"We dive!" said the four,
So they dived and they burrowed,
In the reeds on the shore.

Over in the meadow,
In a snug beehive,
Lived a mother honey bee,
And her little bees five,
"Buzz!" said the mother;
"We buzz!" said the five,
So they buzzed and they hummed,
In the snug beehive.

Over in the meadow,
In a nest built of sticks,
Lived a black mother crow,
And her little crows six,
"Caw!" said the mother;
"We caw!" said the six,
So they cawed and they called,
In their nest built of sticks.

Over in the meadow,
Where the grass is so even,
Lived a gay mother cricket,
And her little crickets seven,
"Chirp!" said the mother;
"We chirp!" said the seven,
So they chirped cheery notes,
In the grass soft and even.

Over in the meadow,
By the old mossy gate,
Lived a brown mother lizard,
And her little lizards eight,
"Bask!" said the mother;
"We bask!" said the eight,
So they basked in the sun,
On the old mossy gate.

Over in the meadow,
Where the quiet pools shine,
Lived a green mother frog,
And her little froggies nine,
"Croak!" said the mother;
"We croak!" said the nine,
So they croaked and they splashed,
Where the quiet pools shine.

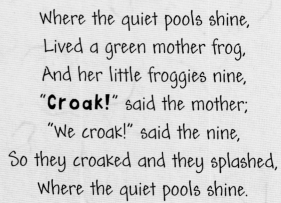

Over in the meadow,
In a sly little den,
Lived a grey mother spider,
And her little spiders ten,
"Spin!" said the mother;
"We spin!" said the ten,
So they spun lacy webs,
In their sly little den.

Olive A Wadsworth

Hospitality

Said a Snake to a Frog with a wrinkled skin,
"As I notice, dear, that your dress is thin,
And a rain is coming, I'll take you in."

John Bannister Tabb

The Dog

Here is the Dog. Since time began,
The Dog has been the friend of man,
The Dog loves man because he shears
His coat and clips his tail and ears.
Man loves the Dog because he'll stay
And listen to his talk all day,
And wag his tail and show delight
At all his jokes, however trite.
His bark is far worse than his bite,
So people say. They may be right;
Yet if to make a choice I had,
I'd choose his bark, however bad.

Oliver Herford

From A Make Believe

I will think as thinks the rabbit:
Let the wind chafe
In the trees overhead,
We are quite safe
In our dark, yellow bed!
Let the rain pour!
It never can bore
A hole in our roof —
It is waterproof!
So is the cloak
We always carry,
We furry folk,
In sandhole or
    quarry!

It is perfect bliss
To lie in a nest
So soft as this,
All so warmly drest!
No one to flurry you!
No one to hurry you!
No one to scurry you!
Holes plenty to creep in!
All day to sleep in!
All night to roam in!
Grey dawn to run home in!
And all the days and nights to
come after —
All the tomorrows for hind-legs
and laughter!

George Macdonald

Bird Songs

I will sing a song,
Said the owl.
You sing a song, sing-song
Ugly fowl!
What will you sing about,
Night in and day out?

All about the night,
When the grey
With her cloak smothers bright,
Hard, sharp day.
Oh, the moon! The cool dew!
And the shadows! — **tu-whoo!**

I will sing a song,
Said the nightingale.
Sing a song, long, long,
Little Neverfail!
What will you sing about,
Day in or day out?

All about the light
Gone away,
Down, away, and out of sight:
Wake up, day!
For the master is not dead,
Only gone to bed.

I will sing a song,
Said the lark.
Sing, sing, Throat-strong,
Little Kill-the-dark!
What will you sing about,
Day in and night out?

I can only call!
I can't think!
Let me up, that's all!
I see a chink!
I've been thirsting all night
For the glorious light!

George Macdonald

A Friend in the Garden

He is not John the gardener,
And yet the whole day long
Employs himself most usefully,
The flowerbeds among.

He is not Tom the pussy-cat,
And yet the other day,
With stealthy stride and glistening eye,
He crept upon his prey.

He is not Dash the dear old dog,
And yet, perhaps, if you
Took pains with him and petted him,
You'd come to love him too.

He's not a Blackbird, though he chirps,
And though he once was black;
And now he wears a loose grey coat,
All wrinkled on the back.

He's got a very dirty face,
And very shining eyes!
He sometimes comes and sits indoors;
He looks – and p'r'aps is – wise.

But in a sunny flowerbed
He has his fixed abode;
He eats the things that eat my plants –
He is a friendly **TOAD**.

Juliana Horatia Ewing

Toads are very popular with gardeners because they eat slugs and beetles, which would otherwise eat the plants.

What Became of Them?

He was a rat, and she was a rat,
And down in one hole they did dwell,
And both were as black as a witch's cat,
And they loved one another well.

He had a tail, and she had a tail,
Both long and curling and fine;
And each said, "Yours is the finest tail
In the world, excepting mine."

He smelt the cheese, and she smelt the cheese,
And they both pronounced it good;
And both remarked it would greatly add
To the charms of their daily food.

So he ventured out, and she ventured out,
And I saw them go with pain;
But what befell them I never can tell,
For they never came back again.

Anonymous

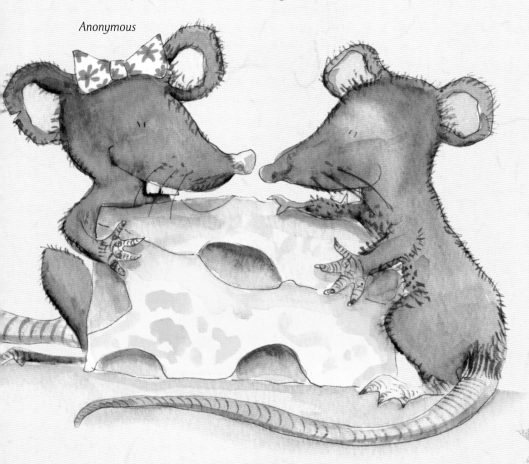

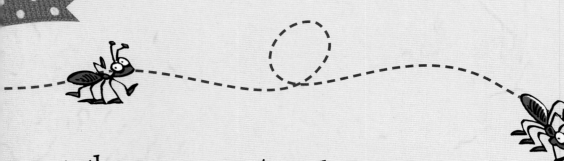

The Ant Explorer

Once a little sugar ant made up his mind to roam —
To far away far away, far away from home.
He had eaten all his breakfast, and he had his ma's consent
To see what he should chance to see and here's the way he went —
Up and down a fern frond, round and round a stone,
Down a gloomy gully, where he loathed to be alone,
Up a mighty mountain range, seven inches high,
Through the fearful forest grass that nearly hid the sky,
Out along a bracken bridge, bending in the moss,
Till he reached a dreadful desert that was feet and feet across.

'Twas a dry, deserted desert, and a trackless land to tread;
 He wished that he was home again and tucked up tight in bed.
His little legs were wobbly, his strength was nearly spent,
And so he turned around again and here's the way he went —
Back along a bracken bridge, bending in the moss,
Through the fearful forest grass shutting out the sky,
Up a mighty mountain range, seven inches high,
Down a gloomy gully, where he loathed to be alone,
Up and down a fern frond, round and round a stone.
A dreary ant, a weary ant, resolved no more to roam,
He staggered up the garden path and popped back home.

C J Dennis

The Fox

The Fox went out one winter night,
And prayed the moon to give him light,
For he'd many a mile to go that night,
Before he reached his den, O!
Den, O! Den, O!
For he'd many a mile to go that night,
For he'd many a mile to go that night,
Before he reached his den, O!

At last he came to a farmer's yard,
Where the ducks and the geese were all afear'd
"The best of you all shall grease my beard,
Before I leave the Town O!
Town O! Town O!
The best of you all shall grease my beard,
The best of you all shall grease my beard,
Before I leave the Town O!

He took the grey goose by the neck,
He laid a duck across his back,
And heeded not their quack! quack! quack!
The legs of all dangling down, O!
Down, O! Down O!
And heeded not their quack! quack! quack!
And heeded not their quack! quack! quack!
The legs of all dangling down, O!

Then old mother Slipper Slopper jump'd out of bed
And out of the window she pop't her head,
Crying "Oh! John, John! the grey goose is dead,
And the fox is over the down, O!"
Down, O! Down O!
Crying "Oh! John, John! the grey goose is dead,
Crying "Oh! John, John! the grey goose is dead,
And the fox is over the down, O!"

Then John got up to the top
    o' the hill,
And blew this horn both loud
    and shrill,
"Blow on" said Reynard,
    "your music still,
Whilst I trot home to my den, O",
Den, O! Den, O!,
"Blow on" said Reynard, "your
    music still,
"Blow on" said Reynard, "your music still,
Whilst I trot home to my den, O",

At last he came to his cosy den,
Where sat his young ones, nine or ten,
Quoth they, "Daddy, you must go there again,
For sure, 'tis a lucky town, O!"
Town, O! Town, O!
Quoth they, "Daddy, you must go there again,
Quoth they, "Daddy, you must go there again,
For sure, 'tis a lucky town, O!"

The fox and wife without any strife,
   They cut up the goose without fork or knife,
   And said 'twas the best they had eat in their life,
   And the young ones pick'd the bones, O!
Bones, O! Bones, O!
And said 'twas the best they had eat in their life,
And said 'twas the best they had eat in their life,
And the young ones pick'd the bones, O!

Anonymous

What is Pink?

What is pink? A rose is pink
By the fountain's brink.
What is red? A poppy's red
In its barley bed.
What is blue? The sky is blue
Where the clouds float through.
What is white? A swan is white
Sailing in the light.
What is yellow? Pears are yellow,
Rich and ripe and mellow.
What is green? The grass is green,
With small flowers between.
What is violet? Clouds are violet
In the summer twilight.
What is orange? Why, an orange,
Just an orange!

Christina Rossetti

From To a Butterfly

Oh! Pleasant, pleasant were the days,
The time, when, in our childish plays,
My sister Emmeline and I
Together chased the butterfly!
A very hunter did I rush
Upon the prey — with leaps and springs
I followed on from brake to bush;
But she, God love her, feared to brush
The dust from off its wings.

William Wordsworth

Brake a small
clump of trees

Milk for the Cat

When the tea is brought at five o'clock,
And all the neat curtains are drawn with care,
The little black cat with bright green eyes
Is suddenly purring there.
At first she pretends, having nothing to do,
She has come in merely to blink by the grate,
But, though tea may be late or the milk may be sour,
She is never late.
And presently her agate eyes
Take a soft large milky haze,
And her independent casual glance
Becomes a stiff, hard gaze.
Then she stamps her claws or
    lifts her ears,
Or twists her tail and begins
    to stir,
Till suddenly all her lithe
    body becomes
One breathing, trembling purr.

The children eat and wriggle and laugh;
The two old ladies stroke their silk:
But the cat is grown small and thin with desire,
Transformed to a creeping lust for milk.
The white saucer like some full moon descends
At last from the clouds of the table above;
She sighs and dreams and thrills and glows,
Transfigured with love.

She nestles over the shining rim,
Buries her chin in the creamy sea;
Her tail hangs loose; each drowsy paw
Is doubled under each bending knee.
A long, dim ecstasy holds her life;
Her world is an infinite shapeless white,
Till her tongue has curled the last holy drop,
Then she sinks back into the night,
Draws and dips her body to heap
Her sleepy nerves in the great arm-chair,
Lies defeated and buried deep
Three or four hours unconscious there.

Harold Monro

Dapple-Grey

I had a little pony,
His name was Dapple-Grey,
I lent him to a lady,
To ride a mile away.
She whipped him, she slashed him,
She rode him through the mire;
I would not lend my pony now
For all the lady's hire.

Anonymous

Donkey

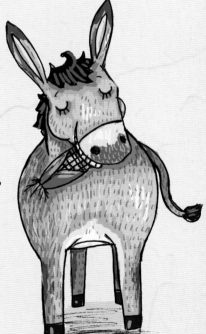

If I had a donkey that wouldn't go,
Would I beat him? Oh, no, no.
I'd put him in the barn and give
    him some corn.
The best little donkey that ever
    was born.

Anonymous

The Flowers

All the names I know from nurse:
Gardener's garters, Shepherd's purse,
Bachelor's buttons, Lady's smock,
And the Lady Hollyhock.

Fairy places, fairy things,
Fairy woods where the wild bee wings,
Tiny trees for tiny dames,
These must all be fairy names!

Tiny woods below whose boughs
Shady fairies weave a house;
Tiny tree-tops, rose or thyme,
Where the braver fairies climb!

Fair are grown-up people's trees,
But the fairest woods are these;
Where, if I were not so tall,
I should live for good and all.

Robert Louis Stevenson

Squirrel

Whisky Frisky,
Hippity hop,
Up he goes
To the tree-top!

Whirly, twirly,
Round and round,
Down he scampers
To the ground.

Furly, curly,
What a tail!
Tall as a feather,
Broad as a sail!

Where's his supper?
In the shell,
Snappy, cracky,
Out it fell!

Anonymous

To a Squirrel at Kyle-Na-No

Come play with me;
Why should you run
Through the shaking tree
As though I'd a gun
To strike you dead?
When all I would do
Is to scratch your head
And let you go.

W B Yeats

Robin Redbreast

Goodbye, goodbye to Summer!
For Summer's nearly done;
The garden smiling faintly,
Cool breezes in the sun;
Our Thrushes now are silent,
Our Swallows flown away –
Hang russet on the bough,
It's Autumn, Autumn, Autumn late,
'Twill soon be winter now.
Robin, Robin Redbreast,
O Robin dear!

And what will this poor Robin do?
For pinching days are near.

The fireside for the Cricket,
The wheatsack for the Mouse,
When trembling night-winds whistle
And moan all round the house;
The frosty ways like iron,
The branches plumed with snow –
Alas! In Winter, dead, and dark,
Where can poor Robin go?
Robin, Robin Redbreast,
O Robin dear!
And a crumb of bread for Robin,
His little heart to cheer.

William Allingham

Growing Up

Little Tommy Tadpole began to weep and wail,
For little Tommy Tadpole had lost his little tail;
And his mother didn't know him as he wept upon a log,
For he wasn't Tommy Tadpole, but Mr Thomas Frog.

C J Dennis

The Robin

When father takes his spade to dig,
Then Robin comes along.
He sits upon a little twig
And sings a little song.

Or, if the trees are rather far,
He does not stay alone,
But comes up close to where we are
And bobs upon a stone.

Laurence Alma-Tadema

The Camel's Complaint

Canary-birds feed on sugar and seed,
Parrots have crackers to crunch;
And, as for the poodles, they tell me the noodles
Have chickens and cream for their lunch.
But there's never a question
About **MY** digestion –
ANYTHING does for me!

Cats, you're aware, can repose in a chair,
Chickens can roost upon rails;
Puppies are able to sleep in a stable,
And oysters can slumber in pails.
But no one supposes a poor camel dozes –
ANY PLACE does for me!

Lambs are enclosed where it's never exposed,
Coops are constructed for hens;
Kittens are treated to houses well-heated,
And pigs are protected by pens.

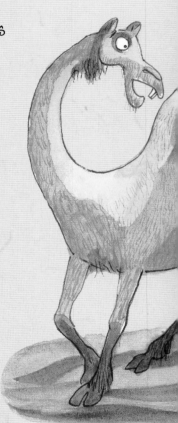

But a Camel comes handy
Wherever it's sandy –
   ANYWHERE does for me!

    People would laugh if you rode a giraffe,
    Or mounted the back of an ox;
    It's nobody's habit to ride on a rabbit,
    Or try to bestraddle a fox.
But as for a Camel, he's
Ridden by families –
   ANY LOAD does for me!

    A snake is as round as a hole in the ground,
    And weasels are wavy and sleek;
    And no alligator could ever be straighter
    Than lizards that live in a creek.
But a Camel's all lumpy
And bumpy and humpy –
   ANY SHAPE does for me!

Charles E Carryl

Kitten's Complaint

In Winter when the air is chill,
And winds are blowing loud and shrill,
All snug and warm I sit and purr,
Wrapped in my overcoat of fur.
In Summer quite the other way,
I find it very hot all day,
But Human People do not care,
For they have nice thin clothes to wear.
And does it not seem hard to you,
When all the world is like a stew,
And I am much too warm to purr,
I have to wear my Winter Fur?

Oliver Herford

Commissariat Camels

We haven't a camelty tune of our own
To help us trollop along,
But every neck is a hair-trombone
(Rtt-ta-ta-ta! is a hair-trombone!)
And this is our marching-song:

Can't! Don't! Shan't! Won't!

Pass it along the line!
Somebody's pack has slid from his back,
Wish it were only mine!
Somebody's load has tipped off in the road –
Cheer for a halt and a row!

Urrr! Yarrh! Grr! Arrh!

Somebody's catching it now!

Rudyard Kipling

Commissariat a system for supplying an army with food

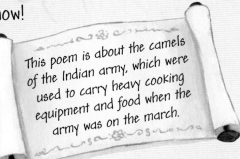

This poem is about the camels of the Indian army, which were used to carry heavy cooking equipment and food when the army was on the march.

An Autumn Greeting

"Come, little leaves,"
Said the wind one day,
"Come over the meadows
With me, and play;
Put on your dresses
Of red and gold;
Summer is gone,
And the days grow cold."

Soon as the leaves
Heard the wind's loud call,
Down they came fluttering,
One and all;
Over the meadows
They danced and flew,
Singing the soft
Little songs they knew.

Dancing and flying
The little leaves went;
Winter had called them
And they were content –
Soon fast asleep
In their earthy beds,
The snow laid a soft mantle
Over their heads.

George Cooper

The South Wind

The south wind brings wet weather;
The north wind wet and cold together;
The west wind always brings us rain;
The east wind blows it back again.

Anonymous

Pigeon's Song

Curr dhoo, curr dhoo,
Love me, and I'll love you!

Anonymous

The Quiet Snow

The quiet snow
Will splotch
Each in the row of cedars
With a fine
And patient hand;
Numb the harshness,
Tangle of that swamp.
It does not say, the sun
Does these things another way.

Even on hats of walkers,
The air of noise
And street-car ledges
It does not know
There should be hurry.

Raymond Knister

Winter

When icicles hang by the wall
And Dick the shepherd blows his nail
And Tom bears logs into the hall,
And milk comes frozen home in pail,
When blood is nipped and ways be foul,
Then nightly sings the staring owl,
Tu-who;
Tu-whit, tu-who: a merry note,
While greasy Joan doth keel the pot.
When all aloud the wind doth blow,
And coughing drowns the parson's saw,
And birds sit brooding in the snow,
And Marian's nose looks red and raw
When roasted crabs hiss in the bowl,
Then nightly sings the staring owl,
Tu-who;
Tu-whit, tu-who: a merry note,
While greasy Joan doth keel the pot.

William Shakespeare

Keel scrub
Parson's saw the sermon
Roasted crabs crabapples
in a bowl of punch

Dandelion

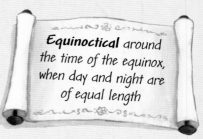

"At my time of life," said the Dandelion,
  "I keep an eye on
The slightest sign of disturbance and riot,
For my one object is to keep quiet
The reason I take such very great care,"
The old Dandy went on, "is because of my hair.
It was very thick once, and as yellow as gold;
  But now I am old,
  It is snowy-white,
  And comes off with the slightest fright.
  As to using a brush
  My good dog! I beseech you, don't rush,
  Go quietly by me, if you please
  You're as bad as a breeze.
I hope you'll attend to what we've said;
And – whatever you do – don't touch my head,
In this equinoctial, blustering weather
You might knock it off with a feather."

Juliana Horatia Ewing

The Dandelion

O dandelion, rich and haughty,
King of village flowers!
Each day is coronation time,
You have no humble hours.
I like to see you bring a troop
To beat the blue-grass spears,
To scorn the lawn-mower that would be
Like fate's triumphant shears,
Your yellow heads are cut away,
It seems your reign is o'er.
By noon you raise a sea of stars
More golden than before.

Vachel Lindsay

The Wind has such a Rainy Sound

The wind has such a rainy sound,
Moaning through the town,
The sea has such a windy sound,
Will the ships go down?
The apples in the orchard
Tumble from their tree.
Oh will the ships go down, go down,
In the windy sea?

Christina Rossetti

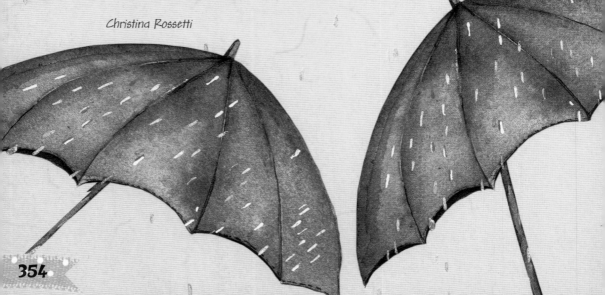

A Toadstool Comes up in a Night

A toadstool comes up in a night,
Learn the lesson, little folk:
An oak grows on a hundred years,
But then it is an oak.

Christina Rossetti

Autumn Greeting

"Come," said the Wind to the Leaves one day.
"Come over the meadow and we will play.
Put on your dresses of red and gold.
For summer is gone and the days grow cold."

Anonymous

From **No**

No sun – no moon!
No morn – no noon –
No dawn – no dusk – no proper time of day.
No warmth, no cheerfulness, no healthful ease,
No comfortable feel in any member –
No shade, no shine, no butterflies, no bees,
No fruits, no flowers, no leaves, no birds! –

No-vember!

Thomas Hood

Member any
body part

November Night

Listen. . .
With faint dry sound,
Like steps of passing ghosts,
The leaves, frost-crisp'd, break from the trees
And fall.

Adelaide Crapsey

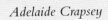

The Sea

The sea! The sea! The open sea!
The blue, the fresh, the ever free!
Without a mark, without a bound,
It runneth the earth's wide regions round;
It plays with the clouds; it mocks the skies;
Or like a cradled creature lies.

I'm on the sea! I'm on the sea!
I am where I would ever be;
With the blue above, and the blue below,
And silence wheresoe'er I go;
If a storm should come and awake the deep,
What matter? I shall ride and sleep.

I love, O, how I love to ride
On the fierce, foaming, bursting tide,
When every mad wave drowns the moon
Or whistles aloft his tempest tune,
And tells how goeth the world below,
And why the sou'west blasts do blow.

I never was on the dull, tame shore,
But I lov'd the great sea more and more,
And backwards flew to her billowy breast,
Like a bird that seeketh its mother's nest;
And a mother she was, and is, to me;
For I was born on the open sea!

The waves were white, and red the morn,
In the noisy hour when I was born;
And the whale it whistled, the porpoise roll'd,
And the dolphins bared their backs of gold;
And never was heard such an outcry wild
As welcom'd to life the ocean-child!

I've liv'd since then, in calm and strife,
Full fifty summers, a sailor's life,
With wealth to spend and a power to range,
But never have sought nor sighed for change;
And Death, whenever he comes to me
Shall come on the wild, unbounded sea!

Barry Cornwall

I am his Highness' Dog

I am his Highness' dog at Kew;
Pray tell me sir, whose dog
are you?

Alexander Pope

Alexander Pope, wrote
this poem when the Prince
Regent, son of King George
III, asked him for a poem
for his dog's collar.

The Sea

Behold the wonders
of the deep,
Where crabs and lobsters
learn to creep,
And little fishes
learn to swim,
And clumsy sailors
tumble in.

Anonymous

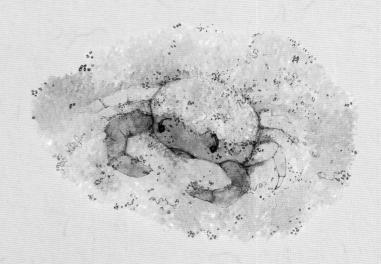

From # The Stars

Look at the stars! Look, look up at the skies!
O look at all the fire-folk sitting in the air!
The bright boroughs, the circle-citadels there!
Down in dim woods the diamond
delves! the elves'-eyes!
The grey lawns cold where gold, where
quickgold lies!

Gerard Manley Hopkins

The Donkey

I saw a donkey one day old,
His head was too big
for his neck to hold;
His legs were shaky
and long and loose,
They rocked and staggered
and weren't much use.

He tried to gambol
and frisk a bit,
but he wasn't quite sure
of the trick of it.
His queer little coat
was soft and grey
and curled at his neck
in a lovely way.

His face was wistful
and left no doubt
that he felt life needed
some thinking about.
So he blundered round
in venturesome quest,
and then lay flat on the ground to rest.

He looked so little
and weak and slim,
I prayed the world
might be good to him.

Anonymous

The Snail

The Snail he lives in his hard round house,
In the orchard, under the tree:
Says he, "I have but a single room;
But it's large enough for me."

The snail in his little house doth dwell
All the week from end to end,
You're at home, Master Snail; that's all very well.
But you never receive a friend.

Anonymous

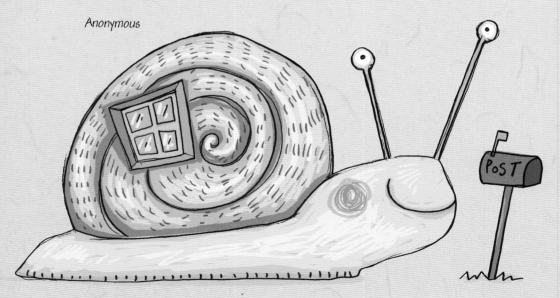

It

A wee little worm in a hickory-nut
Sang, happy as he could be, –
"O I live in the heart of the whole round world,
And it all belongs to me!"

James Whitcomb Riley

Riddle: I have only One Foot

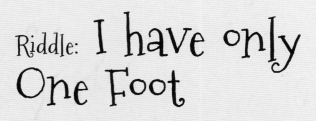

I have only one foot, but thousands of toes;
My one foot stands well, but never goes;
I've a good many arms, if you count them all,
But hundreds of fingers, large and small;
From the ends of my fingers my beauty grows;
I breathe with my hair, and I drink with my toes;
I grow bigger and bigger about the waist
Although I am always very tight laced;
None e'er saw me eat – I've no mouth to bite!
Yet I eat all day, and digest all night.

In the summer, with song I shake and quiver,
But in winter I fast and groan and shiver.

George Macdonald

Answer: a tree

An Emerald is as Green as Grass

An Emerald is as green as grass;
A ruby red as blood;
A sapphire shines as blue as heaven;
A flint lies in the mud.
A diamond is a brilliant stone,
To catch the world's desire;
An opal holds a fiery spark;
But a flint holds fire.

Christina Rossetti

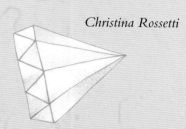

The Little Cock-sparrow

A little cock-sparrow sat on a green tree,
And he chirruped, he chirruped, so merry was he;
A little cock-sparrow sat on a green tree,
And he chirruped, he chirruped, so merry was he.

A naughty boy came with his wee bow and arrow,
Determined to shoot this little cock-sparrow.
A naughty boy came with his wee bow and arrow,
Determined to shoot this little cock-sparrow.

"This little cock-sparrow shall make me a stew,
And his giblets shall make me a little pie, too."
"Oh, no!" said the sparrow,
    "I won't make a stew."
So he flapped his wings,
    and away he flew.

Anonymous

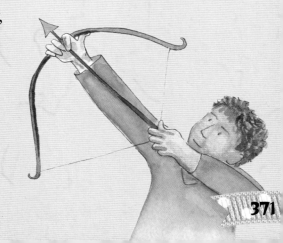

371

Snow

In the gloom of whiteness,
In the great silence of snow,
A child was sighing
And bitterly saying: "Oh,
They have killed a white bird up there on her nest,
The down is fluttering from her breast!"
And still it fell through that dusky brightness
On the child crying for the bird of the snow.

Edward Thomas

Jack Frost

Rustily creak the crickets.
Jack Frost came down last night.
He slid to the earth on a star beam,
Keen and sparkling and bright.

Celia Thaxter

The Wonderful World

Great, wide, beautiful, wonderful World,
With the wonderful water round you curled,
And the wonderful grass upon your breast,
World, you are beautifully dressed.

The wonderful air is over me,
And the wonderful wind is shaking the tree,
It walks on the water, and whirls the mills,
And talks to itself on the top of the hills.

You friendly Earth, how far do you go,
With the wheat fields that nod and the rivers that flow,
With cities and gardens and cliffs and isles,
And the people upon you for thousands of miles?

Ah! You are so great, and I am so small,
I hardly can think of you, World, at all;
And yet, when I said my prayers today,
My mother kissed me, and said, quite gay,

"If the wonderful world is great to you,
And great to Father and Mother, too,
You are more than the Earth, though you are such a dot!
You can love and think, and the Earth cannot!"

William Brighty Rands

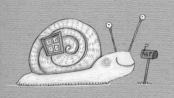

INDEX OF POETS

INDEX OF FIRST LINES

The End